FAST ITALIAN MEALS

FAST ITALIAN MEALS

by Emalee Chapman

book design and illustration
by Alice Harth

101 Productions
San Francisco

Printed and bound in the United States of America.

Distributed to the book trade in the United States
by Charles Scribner's Sons, New York.

Published by 101 Productions
834 Mission Street
San Francisco, California 94103

Library of Congress Cataloging in Publication Data

Chapman, Emalee.
    Fast Italian meals.

    Includes index.
    1.   Cookery, Italian.   I.   Title.
TX723.C49   1983   641.5'55
                                        83-6255
ISBN 0-89286-210-6

CONTENTS

THE FOOD IN ITALY always seems irresistible to me, as it is basically simple, fresh, and natural. There is common sense in the Italian attitude concerning food, a straight-forward enjoyment of good eating. Italian cooking can be fast and adaptable, while inventive, healthful, and inexpensive, exactly what we need for the way we live today.

As I was writing this book, I combined by research with sightseeing and a holiday. I went every day to the outdoor food markets to see the stalls of seasonal fruits, vegetables, cheeses, meats, and fish. The marketplace is alive with activity; it is vibrant, colorful, and exciting. This is where the best and cheapest food is found.

Italian home cooking (and country cooking called *rustica*) comes directly from the local marketplace. This simple cooking relies on fresh foods and uses fast cooking methods that respect and enhance the bright color, taste, and quality of each ingredient. The food tastes as good as it looks, and is as flavorful as the heavenly aroma that fills every Italian kitchen.

Here are my recipes for fast Italian meals, with the emphasis on fresh food, quickly prepared; the meals are meant to be savored slowly and enjoyed. You will be able to combine eating and pleasure when so little time, energy, and money are spent cooking your meals in fifteen minutes or less.

- I have used only those ingredients that are readily available everywhere.
- My recipes take very little time to prepare and are nutritious and good to eat; you have only to select the ingredients carefully.
- All of the recipes make two servings unless stated otherwise. They can be easily increased to serve more, but you must remember to increase the preparation time as well.

METHODS FOR COOKING
FAST ITALIAN MEALS

My methods show you how to be organized in your kitchen: how to save time, energy, and money. The methods incorporate ideas for your waistline and health, as they suggest how to use less salt, meat, and fat in your cooking. Follow these simple methods for meals that require a minimum of preparation, cooking, and cleanup.

● Save minutes by preheating the oven (at least 10 minutes) or putting water on to boil when you walk into the kitchen. Use this time to prepare vegetables, meats, and desserts.

● Wash all fruits and vegetables under tap water before using. Do not peel, as the nutrients are in the skin.

● Slice fruits and coarsely chop vegetables; they will need less cooking liquid, will cook more quickly, and will retain their flavor and vitamins. Use the broth as a sauce.

● Trim fat from meat, fillet and trim fish, and bone, skin, and slice fowl; all will cook more quickly and will be tender and juicy, and some fat is removed from the diet.

● My sauces are thickened by very fast boiling over high heat for a short time. As the sauce reduces, the seasoning becomes more concentrated, so season carefully. I think sauces are best when not cooked too long, so don't boil away the fresh taste and vitamins.

● The Italians are imaginative and realistic in the use of contrasting temperatures for serving foods. I have specified these four different temperatures in my recipes because this approach makes the cooking and serving of meals easier as well as more interesting.

Room temperature and chilled dishes lend themselves to advance preparation, making it possible to cook whenever it is most convenient, and these dishes do not demand the same care and speed in serving as those that are served hot.

Hot: Most pasta and rice dishes, grilled steaks, roasted meats, sautéed and baked fish, meat, and fowl; all are served hot on a warm plate.

Room temperature: Most vegetables, salads, poached fish, egg dishes, lentils, custards, cooked fruits; fruits such as strawberries, raspberries, and pears should be served at room temperature.

Chilled: Summer fruits like grapes, cherries, and melons; cold soups and purée of eggplant; all are served chilled on a cool plate.

Semifrozen (half-frozen) or frozen: Many Italian desserts, ice creams, ices, molded desserts, mousses; all are taken from the refrigerator and served on a chilled plate.

KITCHEN EQUIPMENT:
THE ESSENTIALS FOR FAST COOKING

Here are the basic tools and equipment needed for a completely efficient kitchen. Whether or not space is limited, every item should be carefully chosen for the job it will do: knives of the best quality; heavy pots and pans that retain heat without scorching. Consider this list when planning your well-organized kitchen.

Saucepans, 3: Small, medium, and large; should be heavy in order to evenly distribute heat. Use the large one for cooking pasta, soups.

Sauté pans, 3: Small, medium, and large; use for cooking vegetables, fruits, meats, fowl, fish, rice dishes.

Oven dishes, 3: Earthenware or porcelain; 1 large oval, approximately 9 X 13 inches, for baking, roasting meat, fowl, fish; 1 medium rectangle, approximately 7 X 12 inches, for baked pastas, vegetable puddings; 1 small oval, approximately 6 X 9 inches, for preparing 2 servings, custards, desserts. Buy attractive oven dishes that can go from oven to table.

Mixing bowls, 5: Earthenware or ceramic, in graduated sizes from about 1 cup to 2 quarts; use for soups, salads, sauces, desserts. Use the large bowl for whipping eggs, mixing ingredients.

Oven sheet: Round or rectangular heavy iron sheet; essential for baking, broiling, toasting bread.

Blender: Essential for making soups, sauces, fast meals.

Measuring cup: Two-cup Pyrex.

Measuring spoons

Knives, 4: Chef's, boning, vegetable, and large serrated bread; select good-quality, high-carbon stainless-steel knives with heavy hardwood handles.

Wooden board: For chopping vegetables, pounding meat, slicing bread.

Wooden spoons, 4: Three for stirring and serving, 1 slotted.

Fork, wooden handle: For cooking hot foods.

Spatulas, 2: Rubber spatula for removing foods from bowls, blender; metal for removing hot foods from oven sheet, pans.

Sieve, large: Use as a strainer, sifter, steaming basket, colander.

Whisk or egg beater: For egg whites, yolks, whipped cream, stirring lumps out of sauces.

Grater, upright: For cheese, vegetables.

Can opener

Pepper mill

Corkscrew

Individual oven dishes, 4: Not essential, but handy to have; rectangular 3 X 6-inch earthenware or porcelain dishes for serving antipasto, baking individual custards, vegetable puddings.

BASIC FOODS TO KEEP ON
THE SHELF FOR FAST ITALIAN MEALS

The aroma of the Italian kitchen is different because of the many herbs and special foods used to add flavor in cooking. The Italian seasons with celery, onions, garlic, shallots, and olives; adds a distinct taste with olive oil, prosciutto, sausages, anchovies, and lemon. Spice is added with cloves, nutmeg, saffron, capers, and red pepper; broth, wine, and cheese lend a fragrance to soups and sauces. Here are the essential ingredients to keep on hand for your Italian cooking.

Butter, unsalted: Use only unsalted butter, as it is better for you and will not burn as quickly at high cooking or baking temperatures.

Chicken broth: An important basic in Italian cooking; used instead of water for cooking meats, vegetables, soups, and sauces to add flavor. A quick broth made with bouillon cubes is preferable to using plain water. Beef broth is also sometimes used.

Cream, heavy or whipping: As natural as possible, without additives.

Garlic: A clove of garlic is often added to a dish for seasoning, and removed after the dish is cooked.

Lemon: Essential in Italian cooking; the grated rind and juice are added to salads, vegetables, meats, fowl, and desserts. Lemon is used to garnish.

Mushrooms: Used to intensify the flavor of soups, stews, and pasta sauces. If dried, they must be soaked in liquid before using; can be mixed with fresh mushrooms for more flavor. Italian mushrooms are also available packed in oil

in a jar; sauté them in their own oil with chopped garlic and herbs as a sauce for omelets and pasta; also good when used to sauté meat, chicken, or fish for a fast meal.

Oil, olive: A basic ingredient of the Italian kitchen, but must be used carefully as too much can spoil a dish. Oil, like wine, varies in taste and color from year to year. The best oil comes from the trees that grow on the hills of Tuscany; Sicily produces a heavier, more pungent oil with a strong fragrance of olives. It is important to use a fine, pure oil, especially when the oil adds flavor (salads, raw vegetables, fish soups). Sometimes I specify the combination of oil and butter (as the Italians do) for sautéing meat and fowl because it will withstand more heat without burning. Most olive oil should not be kept for more than a year, and should be stored in a cool, dark place.

Oil, safflower: Should be kept on hand for deep-frying and sautéing foods, and for making a light mayonnaise.

Olives: Green or black olives are good for nibbling with drinks or as a fast antipasto. Finely chopped olives mixed with olive oil and herbs make a savory sauce for pasta, salads, and eggs.

Parmesan cheese: Keep a one-pound piece, well wrapped, in your refrigerator at all times. There is no substitute for Parmesan, and it should always be freshly grated. It is an essential ingredient in soups, and chicken, veal, pasta, and rice dishes. A soft piece of Parmesan makes a delicious snack with bread or fruit.

Pasta: An Italian kitchen is not complete without several types of pasta on the shelf. I always keep packages of shells, penne, spaghetti, and pastina (tiny soup pasta) for fast meals.

Pepper, crushed red: Used in many dishes. A combination of ground red pepper and paprika makes a piquant flavoring.

Peppercorns, black: Freshly ground black pepper is very important in Italian dishes. The Romans adore black pepper; pecorino is sometimes flavored with large black peppercorns or coarsely ground red pepper. A delicious Roman pasta sauce combines olive oil, grated pecorino romano cheese, and freshly ground black pepper.

Peppers, sweet: Red and yellow peppers packed in vinegar will make an instant antipasto, salad, or vegetable dish combined with tomatoes; they also add flavor to meat, chicken, and fish dishes.

Polenta: An imported Italian cornmeal; can be found in packages or bulk in Italian markets and some supermarkets. Polenta makes a complete meal with a vegetable or a salad.

Prosciutto: This pale, rose-colored ham, with edges of opaque, silky-white fat, is best when sliced paper thin. It is so highly flavored it seasons any food it is cooked or combined with; you can see the bone hanging in Italian markets, as Italians save the bone for cooking soups and bean stews. Keep several slices of prosciutto, well wrapped, in your refrigerator for cooking, sandwiches, or to combine with melon, figs, or vegetables as an appetizer.

Rice: The Italian variety is essential for making rice dishes. The Arborio rice of the Po Valley is short and fat; it absorbs broth in cooking without becoming mushy.

Sea salt: When salt is called for, I prefer sea salt, as it provides an interesting texture and flavor, especially in salads.

Tomatoes: When you need fresh, juicy ripe tomatoes and they are not available, canned Italian plum tomatoes are a better choice than tasteless fresh ones. Don't discard the juice from the can; add it to soups, broths, and sauces.

Tuna, canned: Imported Italian solid light tuna, packed in olive oil, is best, and always good to have on hand for an emergency meal. Tuna is used in some pasta sauces, veal dishes, and salads.

Vegetables: Seasonal vegetables are very important in Italian cooking, but when out of season, or limp and tired, use frozen vegetables instead. If you keep artichoke hearts, peas, spinach, broccoli, green beans, and carrots on the freezer shelf, you can always have a fast, nutritious meal.

Vinegar: Italian white wine vinegar gives a light, subtle accent when combined with olive oil for salads and vegetables. Good red wine vinegar comes from Chianti. Always use unflavored wine vinegar. Measure vinegar carefully; too much can spoil a dish.

Wine, for cooking: Wine fit to drink is fit for cooking; I use my leftover opened wine for cooking (dry white wine, champagne). Marsala can be used for veal and poultry dishes and desserts; vermouth lends accent to sauces. The Italians use wine as a seasoning, like herbs and pepper, but not carelessly, as too much wine will spoil the sauce. The dish cooked with wine must be brought to boil to allow the alcohol to evaporate and flavors to blend.

The following foods are not essential, but lend a distinct Italian flavor when used in cooking.

Anchovy fillets, canned: One or two fillets add zest to sauces and salads.

Capers: Used to season and garnish sauces, and chicken, veal, and fish dishes.

Pine nuts: An important addition, for both flavor and texture, to many dishes.

Vinegar, aceto balsamico: An herb-flavored vinegar that is the exception to the use of unflavored wine vinegar; it does not have a sharp bite. Can be served over ripe berries, combined with wine vinegar for a softer flavor in salads, and does not interfere with the drinking of wine when used in an antipasto.

HERBS FOR ITALIAN MEALS

The Italians cherish herbs. Herbs are mentioned often in Roman legends, with great importance placed on their healing powers.

In the open market there are large bouquets of sweetly scented herbs hanging by stems tied with straw; nearby are long braids of garlic and onions. Many varieties of local goat cheese are on display; some are rolled in herbs, fennel, crushed peppercorns, or wrapped in sweet chestnut leaves.

Basil: Considered a love charm in Italy, basil gives spark to salads, soups, meats, egg dishes, pork and lima beans. There is the colorful green *pesto* sauce made of basil, olive oil, and cheese; *pesto rosso* is made of basil, olive oil, and tomatoes. Fresh basil loses its pungency when cooked too long.

Bay leaves (laurel): Italian cooks use a mixture of chopped onion, celery leaves, garlic, tomato, and crumbled bay leaves, all fried in olive oil, to make an aromatic base for soups, stews, and sauces. When grilling skewered meats (liver, sausage), bay leaves are sometimes placed between the pieces of meat to add a subtle flavor.

Fennel: Has the flavor of licorice, a bulbous root like celery, and feathery fernlike leaves. Italians slice it raw for salad and serve it with a sauce of lemon and olive oil. Fennel is used in cooking to flavor fish, chicken, and veal. A stick of fennel is sometimes used as a skewer for grilled meats and fish; fennel stalks are often thrown on a charcoal fire when grilling lamb and fish because they impart a wonderful aroma as the food cooks.

Marjoram: Also known as sweet marjoram; grows in most of the countries bordering on the Mediterranean. Gives flavor to soups, eggs, tomatoes, veal, lamb, cheese dishes, white fish, peas; substitutes nicely for salt and can be used lavishly as a garnish. The oval gray-green leaves are velvety to the touch and make a fragrant tea.

Mint: Used in many Roman dishes; complements fresh fruit, artichokes, fish; steamed zucchini and carrots are served with chopped mint.

Oregano: Italian cooks use this herb in ravioli, pizza, and pasta sauces, in fish and meat dishes; a little goes a long way.

Parsley: Chopped parsley adds a spicy-sweet flavor to soups, vegetables, stews, and pastas. The Italian variety is dark green with a broad, flat leaf. Don't use dried parsley; fresh parsley is always available and keeps well in the refrigerator. Parsley should cook for only a short time, as it will become bitter.

Rosemary: This aromatic herb, a good luck plant for the Italians, has an affinity for poultry, pork, lamb, tomatoes, and seafood. On Capri I saw branches of rosemary dipped into olive oil and used to baste fish; tie a sprig to a small veal or lamb roast.

Sage: This herb with a silvery leaf must be used carefully, as it is strong and can overpower other ingredients. Tuscan cooks use sage in bean soup, white bean dishes, and with pork.

Thyme: Used to scent roast lamb, pork, veal, fowl, beef, and baked or broiled fish. A sprig of thyme placed in a jar of olive oil imparts a delicate flavor.

Remember:
- Herbs are stronger in flavor when dried than when fresh.
- The best way to use dried herbs is to sauté the leaves in warm oil or butter for a few seconds to release the flavor before adding the other ingredients.
- If adding dried herbs to an uncooked dish, such as a salad, crumble them first in the warmth of your hands.
- Herbs can be dried naturally: hang large bunches by their stems in a warm room; place small bunches by the kitchen stove. When dry, transfer the herbs to a glass jar with a cover in order to preserve the scent and flavor.
- Dried herbs are useless if they sit on the shelf too long, as they become tasteless.

CHEESES FOR ITALIAN MEALS

The cooking of Italy relies heavily on cheese as an important ingredient; grated cheese is sprinkled generously on soups, salads, pasta, fowl, and vegetables. Cheese served with fruit usually is dessert; bread and cheese can be a feast with a glass of red wine.

Since every cheese has a distinct flavor, texture, and shape, it is important to know how to recognize and use each one. Here are the classic varieties of Italian cheese imported to the United States, from the creamy, soft cheeses that are as sweet as butter, to the rich and aromatic ones, including the hard (*grana*) types used for both grating and nibbling.

Asiago: A mountain cheese from the Veneto. A firm, lightly flavored cheese made from cow's milk. When young it is a tasty table cheese; as it hardens with age it becomes a sharp grating cheese.

Bel paese: From northern Italy. A mild, semisoft yellow cheese made from pasteurized cow's milk; it is good eaten alone or with fruit. This cheese, with a rich buttery consistency, melts well when used for cooking because of its high-fat content. Try thick slices dipped in beaten egg yolk, rolled in bread crumbs, and fried in butter.

Caciotta: Cacio means local. This cheese is made throughout Italy from cow, goat, and sheep's milk; as it ages the flavor becomes sharper, the texture firmer, and a crust forms on the outside. On Capri caciotta is made in small baskets that leave a textured imprint; a favorite Roman pasta is made with caciotta and black pepper.

Caprini: Generally from the mountainous regions of Italy. Little logs of fresh, soft, creamy goat's milk cheese that are usually marinated in olive oil and black pepper.

Fontina: From Piedmont. A semifirm cheese with a smooth texture made from cow's milk; mild in taste when young, it becomes more piquant with age. Fontina can be identified by its square shape and brown rind. This rich cheese melts well, is delicious when used in cooking, and is excellent for dessert with pears or apples.

Gorgonzola: From northern Italy. This soft, blue-green cow's milk cheese has a rich, smooth creaminess, a delicate and distinctive flavor, and a moist texture. This glorious cheese is divine with fresh pears, can be combined with olives, and makes a savory sauce for gnocchi and pasta.

Mascarpone: Most of the good creamy cow's milk cheeses come from Lombardy, as does this soft cheese. Made with fresh cream, mascarpone is exquisitely delicate, almost like butter; it is often mixed with chopped walnuts, spread on bread, or whipped with sugar, fruit, and liqueur to make a dessert.

Mozzarella: Originally from the region around Naples. Mozzarella is made in large and small sizes; the tiny fresh balls, looking like small peeled eggs, are kept in large bowls of their own "milk." This pure, white buffalo's milk cheese should be eaten fresh and dripping; fresh mozzarella is soft, almost saltless, and coats food gently when cooked. If made with cow's milk, mozzarella is light yellow in color and waxen, and becomes stringy and tough when heated; substitute another bland good-melting cheese (bel paese). Smoked mozzarella has a golden skin.

Parmesan: This hard (*grana*) cheese, also known as Parmigiano Reggiano, is the grating cheese of northern Italy (Parma, Bologna); a good grating cheese should be at least two years old. Made from skimmed cow's milk, this large wheel of pale-yellow cheese has a grainy texture and is crumbly when cut. Aged Parmesan is the supreme grating and cooking cheese; it can be grated as fine as powder or as coarse as cornmeal, melts in a sauce without forming threads, and adds a rich flavor. Parmesan should always be *freshly* grated.

Pecorino: A hard (*grana*) cheese popular in the countryside. Some of the best cheeses in Italy are made from sheep's milk and are known collectively as pecorino. Pecorino is a salty cheese with a sharp bite; good with black olives, coarse bread, and red wine. Pecorino romano, when matured for several years before sale, has a strong flavor; the Romans often use it instead of Parmesan.

Provolone: From southern Italy. This cheese, made from buffalo or cow's milk, has a soft but firm texture, is sometimes smoked, and comes in a variety of sizes and shapes: round, pear shaped, little pigs, large sausages. Provolone should be eaten when fresh, tender, and a pale-yellow color; when aged, it is hard and sharp and should be kept for cooking.

Ricotta: Produced throughout Italy. This milk-white soft cheese with a smooth consistency must be fresh when used for cooking and eating. Ricotta is combined with other ingredients to make salads, gnocchi, and pasta fillings; it is mixed with wine and sugar for a dessert.

In Rome it is made in a large decorated mound. This low-fat cheese is made from cow's milk in the United States, and can be found in plastic containers in most supermarkets.

Taleggio: From Lombardy. A mild, soft cheese with a pungent quality. This is a delightful dessert cheese with fruit.

Remember:
● Buy authentic cheese, not the processed variety, from reputable markets.
● Buy your cheese in one-pound pieces; wrap each piece tightly in a cloth or waxed paper to exclude air and retain moisture; store in the refrigerator.
● Allow cheese to come to room temperature before using; remove from the refrigerator, unwrap, and expose to air. The cheese will regain texture and flavor.

APPETIZERS in Italy are alluring and appealing; what goes into these colorful dishes depends upon the cook and what is in season. Some of the best eating places in Italy are small unassuming restaurants, usually family owned and managed; they are memorable because of the array of appetizers arranged and displayed on a table by the door when you enter.

An appetizer can be a huge hunk of Parmesan cheese with a sharp knife stuck into it; a bouquet of celery; figs or other fresh fruit with prosciutto; small fish; an assortment of shellfish; both raw and cooked vegetables—mushrooms, fennel, radishes, endive; or a mound of puréed tuna, tomatoes, and potatoes. There is also the hot appetizer: rounds of fried toast spread with a chicken liver sauce.

A few bites of one or two of these dishes with a glass of wine stimulates the appetite for what is to come; the combination of two or three of these dishes makes a simple meal with very little cooking.

ASSORTED VEGETABLES WITH SAUCE

This sauce is delicious with fennel, mushrooms, radishes; try any vegetable in season.

1 cup crème fraîche (homemade, following) or heavy cream
1 teaspoon anchovy paste
1 teaspoon Dijon mustard
1 lemon
Freshly ground black pepper
2 small carrots
3 inner celery stalks
Inner leaves of lettuce or endive

1. In a bowl combine crème fraîche, anchovy paste, and mustard; squeeze in juice of lemon. Stir and season to taste with pepper; refrigerate until ready to serve.
2. Slice carrots and celery; arrange with lettuce leaves on a serving plate with bowl of sauce.
Serves 2.

CREME FRAICHE

1 cup heavy cream
1 tablespoon buttermilk

1. Combine cream and buttermilk in a jar. Cover jar and shake well for 1 minute.
2. Let mixture stand in jar at room temperature for several hours. Store in the refrigerator; it will keep 2–3 weeks.
Makes 1 cup.

BLACK OLIVES WITH LEMON SLICES

Across the Tiber in Trastevere, the ancient towers and buildings with classical stone entrances reflect the golden, glowing ochre tones of old Rome. There are many neighborhood restaurants with good rustic food; they all have gardens for warm-weather dining. We enjoyed this appetizer as a prelude to our meal.

1 cup black olives, pitted
2 tablespoons olive oil
1 lemon
Crushed red pepper

1. Combine olives and oil in a bowl, tossing with a spoon to mix well.
2. Slice unpeeled lemon very thin. Add to bowl and mix with olives and oil.
3. Place on a shallow dish; season to taste with red pepper. Serve at room temperature with coarse crusty bread. Serves 2.

ROMAN TOMATO APPETIZER

I was invited one evening to a studio within the ancient walls of Rome where an Italian sculptor lives. We ate around the open hearth in an enormous room filled with larger-than-life-size chiseled figures.

4 slices coarse white bread
2 unpeeled ripe tomatoes, or 2 canned
   Italian plum tomatoes, drained
6 parsley sprigs (no stems)
2 tablespoons olive oil
1/4 cup grated Parmesan or diced
   mozzarella cheese
2 tablespoons capers, drained
Crushed red pepper
1 garlic clove, peeled

Preheat oven to 400°F
1. Toast bread in *preheated* oven until crisp and golden.
2. Put tomatoes and parsley in a blender and coarsely purée.
3. Heat 1 tablespoon oil in a sauté pan, add tomato mixture, and cook over medium heat for 4–5 minutes, or until no liquid remains; do not overcook.
4. Place hot tomato mixture in a bowl and stir in cheese and capers; season to taste with red pepper. Mixture should be spicy.
5. Cut garlic clove in half and rub over toast; brush toast with 1 tablespoon oil. Spoon tomato mixture on toast and serve at room temperature.
Serves 2.

Note: Tomatoes should not be cooked too long, as they lose their bright color and taste.

MOZZARELLA APPETIZER

4 thick slices mozzarella cheese
1 egg
2 tablespoons water
3 tablespoons all-purpose flour
1/2–1 cup safflower oil

1. Cut cheese into 1-inch squares.
2. Mix egg and water in a bowl; put flour on a piece of waxed paper.
3. Dip cheese squares in egg mixture, then roll in flour to coat all sides.
4. Heat oil in a small saucepan (the smallest pan you have, as the oil must be deep enough to cover the cheese). Test oil temperature with a small square of bread; when it browns quickly, the oil is ready.
5. Place cheese squares in hot oil, a few at a time, and cook 1–2 minutes until golden and crisp. Lift out with a slotted spoon or fork and drain on a paper towel.
6. Serve hot with toothpicks.
Serves 2.

EGGPLANT
WITH RED PEPPERS CAPRI

The natives pass through the main piazza constantly with carts and small wagons bearing produce and baggage into the narrow streets; no automobile or horse and wagon can go beyond this area. At dawn crates of red peppers, purple eggplants, and tomatoes of all shapes and sizes arrive in heavily laden boats. They are unloaded and piled high in the piazza; each box of tomatoes has a long sprig of fresh basil lying on top.

2 tablespoons olive oil
1 teaspoon dried basil
1 sweet red pepper (or 1/2 cup in vinegar in a jar, drained)
1/2 unpeeled small eggplant (about 1 cup chopped)
1 tablespoon red wine vinegar
2 tablespoons capers, drained
Crushed red pepper

1. Heat oil in a sauté pan over medium heat, add basil, and stir a few seconds to flavor oil.
2. With a chef's knife, chop sweet red pepper coarsely; add to pan and stir a few seconds.
3. Chop the eggplant and stir into pan. Cover and cook slowly for 5–6 minutes until vegetables are soft.
4. Stir vinegar and capers into pan, combining with vegetables; season to taste with crushed red pepper.
5. Cook uncovered over medium heat for 4 minutes. Serve at room temperature with coarse crusty bread.
Serves 2.

RED AND YELLOW PEPPERS

As we drove south to Naples, the hills seemed to rise and the road twisted; you could see the cliffs drop to the sea, white stone houses built into the hill-sides, castle ruins and towers. Good local food is highly seasoned and cooked with bright yellow and red peppers, tomatoes, and eggplant.

1/4 cup olive oil
1/2 cup sweet red and yellow peppers, drained*
2 unpeeled ripe tomatoes, or 2 canned Italian plum tomatoes, drained
Crushed red pepper
5 parsley sprigs (no stems)

1. Heat oil in a sauté pan over medium heat. With a chef's knife, chop sweet peppers coarsely, add to oil, and stir a few seconds.
2. Slice tomatoes into pan; stir and cook with peppers over medium heat for 5 minutes. Season to taste with crushed red pepper.
3. Chop parsley and sprinkle on top of cooked vegetables. Serve at room temperature.
Serves 2.

* Sweet red and yellow peppers can be found in 9-ounce jars in vinegar on the market shelf.

BAKED STUFFED MUSHROOMS

4 unpeeled large fresh mushrooms
3 parsley sprigs (no stems)
2 thin slices prosciutto
1/4 cup grated Parmesan cheese
1 tablespoon unsalted butter
1/4 cup chicken broth or dry white wine
Paprika
1 slice coarse white bread

Preheat oven to 375°F
1. Remove stems from mushrooms and place caps, hollow sides up, in an oven dish.
2. Chop stems, parsley, and prosciutto. Combine with grated cheese and mix well.
3. Fill mushroom caps with chopped mixture, add butter to dish, and place in *preheated* oven.
4. After 5 minutes, remove from oven, add broth to bottom of dish, and baste mushrooms; season to taste with paprika.
5. Return dish to oven and cook for 8–9 minutes, basting once.
6. Cut bread slice into quarters and toast in oven until crisp and golden. Place a mushroom on each toast square and serve hot.
Serves 2.

SICILIAN TOMATOES

Sicily sits in the middle of the Mediterranean: vulnerable to invasion, it has a complex history of cultures and a rich mix of customs, language, architecture, and foods. The countryside is beautiful and full of contrasts; there are remnants of early conquerors in the Byzantine and Spanish cathedrals, Moorish palazzos, and the Greek amphitheatre. Along the waterfront, shops sell exotic fish and seashells.

1 tablespoon olive oil
3 unpeeled ripe tomatoes, or 3 canned
    Italian plum tomatoes, drained
1 sweet red pepper (or 1/2 cup in
    vinegar in a jar, drained)
1/2 cup black olives, pitted

1. Heat oil in a sauté pan over medium heat. Slice tomatoes into pan, cover, and cook for about 5 minutes until soft.
2. With a chef's knife, chop pepper coarsely and add to pan with olives; cook uncovered over high heat for 5 minutes to thicken.
3. Serve at room temperature.
Serves 2.

COUNTRY OMELET

Sicilian food is simple and fresh, never more than a few hours old. We ate outside in the warm spring sunshine and clear air; we enjoyed a seafood salad with this omelet. There was a spectacular view of Mount Etna and the sea.

2 slices soft white bread
3 large eggs, at room temperature
1/2 cup milk
1/2 cup grated Parmesan cheese
1 tablespoon olive oil
Freshly ground black pepper

1. Tear bread in pieces into a blender and blend to make coarse crumbs.
2. Break eggs into a bowl and mix lightly with a whisk or egg beater; stir in milk, bread crumbs, and grated cheese.
3. Heat a medium-size omelet pan or sauté pan. When a drop of water dances on the surface, it is ready. Quickly add oil and tilt pan to spread it evenly over surface.
4. Pour in egg mixture. As omelet sets, lift edges with a fork and tilt pan to let uncooked egg flow under. Cook gently over medium-low heat until cooked on bottom but soft in center, about 2 minutes.
5. Loosen omelet with a spatula and slide onto a plate. Cut into wedges and serve at room temperature.
Serves 2.

Try this with Sicilian Tomatoes.

ARTICHOKES MILANESE

4 artichoke bottoms (canned or frozen;
   rinse if packed in vinegar)
1 tablespoon unsalted butter
1/4 cup grated mozzarella or fontina
   cheese
1/4 cup chicken broth
Freshly ground black pepper

Preheat oven to 400°F
1. Place artichoke bottoms, hollow sides
up, in an oven dish. Put a dot of butter
in center of each and sprinkle with
cheese. Pour broth into bottom of dish.
2. Place artichokes in *preheated* oven
for 10 minutes, basting 1–2 times with
broth.
3. Season to taste with pepper and
serve hot.
Serves 2.

CROSTINI

Crostini appears frequently on menus
in Florence served warm on toast at the
start of a meal.

2 slices coarse white bread
1 tablespoon unsalted butter
1/2 teaspoon dried sage
6 chicken livers
3 anchovy fillets, or 2 teaspoons
   anchovy paste (optional)
1 tablespoon capers, drained

Preheat oven to 400°F
1. Cut each bread slice into quarters;
toast in *preheated* oven until crisp and
golden.
2. Melt butter in a sauté pan over
medium heat, add sage, and stir a few
seconds to flavor butter.
3. Stir chicken livers into pan and cook
for 3–4 minutes, turning once, until
brown on the outside and pink in the
center.
4. Stir livers and all pan juices into a
blender. Add anchovies and capers and
blend until a creamy purée.
5. Spread liver purée on toast and
serve warm.
Serves 2.

PRAWNS WITH BASIL

In the Sicilian street market the fish stall has giant swordfish propped up with the long "swords" in the air; there are boxes of small silver fish, and baskets of shellfish garnished with fresh herbs and lemons.

2 tablespoons olive oil
1/2 cup fresh basil leaves, or
   3 tablespoons dried basil
1/2 pound raw prawns, cleaned (leave
   tails on)
2 tablespoons dry white vermouth
Sea salt
Freshly ground black pepper
1 lemon

1. Heat oil in a sauté pan over medium heat, add basil, and stir a few seconds to flavor oil.
2. Stir prawns into pan; pour in vermouth and season to taste.
3. Squeeze juice of lemon into pan and cook prawns about 3 minutes until they turn pink.
4. Serve prawns hot on toothpicks.
Serves 2.

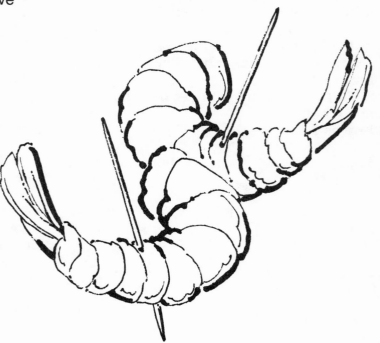

EGGS WITH PARSLEY SAUCE

10 parsley sprigs
8 green olives, pitted
1 garlic clove, peeled (optional)
1 lemon
1/4 cup olive oil
Freshly ground black pepper
4 inner lettuce leaves
2 hard-cooked eggs, peeled

1. Place parsley, olives, and garlic in a blender; squeeze in juice of lemon and purée.
2. With motor running, slowly add oil in a thin stream.
3. Pour sauce into a bowl; season to taste with pepper.
4. Arrange lettuce leaves on a serving plate. Cut eggs in half lengthwise and place on lettuce. Spoon 1 tablespoon sauce over each egg. Serve at room temperature with remaining sauce at table.
Serves 2.

DEVILED CHESTNUTS

This unusual appetizer comes from Verona; it is delightful with a glass of dry white wine. On the way to Verona is an enchanting medieval town with a castle fortress at its entrance. A steep road is fringed with pink oleanders. We drove past the ruins of a magnificent Roman villa with sixteenth-century gardens and a spectacular view.

1 tablespoon unsalted butter
1/2 cup peeled chestnuts, drained
  (available in 10-ounce cans)
Crushed red pepper
2 tablespoons milk

1. Melt butter in a sauté pan over medium heat; stir in drained chestnuts, season to taste with red pepper, and cook for 2–3 minutes until golden brown.
2. Add milk to pan and simmer over medium-low heat for 2–3 minutes until milk is reduced and makes a thick sauce.
3. Serve chestnuts hot on toothpicks.
Serves 2.

SOUP can start a meal, and soup can be a whole meal with bread, cheese, and wine. Soup is an easy and satisfying supper for one or two persons after work, as it can be quickly prepared with a few ingredients.

The Italian knows how to make a soup with vegetables, broth, herbs, and a handful of pasta. In Milan a little rice is added to thicken a soup; the Venetian will use cornmeal; in the south it will be pasta; while in Tuscany beans are favored. The soups of the north are lighter and more delicate than those of the south. The Roman will flavor a soup of lentils and tomato with mint; the Neapolitan likes to add red pepper.

The use of broth (beef, chicken, or fish) gives the soup more flavor and substance than water. Homemade broth is best, but in a pinch broth made with a bouillon cube is better than water.

There is always a bowl of grated cheese on the table for each person to spoon into the soup. Italian soups are served in large shallow soup bowls (unless it is a cup of broth) so that the cheese and soup can be stirred into a creamy whole. The cheese thickens and seasons the soup.

Italians like bread, breadsticks, or toasted bread with soup. Sometimes the toast is rubbed with a garlic clove and olive oil, and then sprinkled with cheese.

Remember:
- Bouillon cubes—chicken or beef—are a quick substitute for homemade broth.
- Use leftover vegetables to make soups in the blender in a hurry.
- Always use *freshly* grated cheese.

EASY CHICKEN BROTH

Italians use broth for cooking instead of water in all kinds of dishes. My method for making broth is so fast and easy you can make a small amount of flavorful broth whenever you have bones and scraps of chicken. This unseasoned broth will lend itself to any dish.

Put bones, skin, and trimmings of chicken into a saucepan and add *only enough* water to cover. (Sometimes I add a chicken breast, legs, or wings, and have a meal of poached chicken.) Bring water to boil and simmer over medium heat, uncovered, for 20 minutes. Strain broth into a bowl, cool, and refrigerate until the fat congeals on top; skim and discard fat.

TOASTED BREAD FOR SOUP

4 thick slices coarse white bread
1 garlic clove, peeled
1/4 cup olive oil

Preheat oven to 375°F
1. Place bread in *preheated* oven for 4–5 minutes until crisp and golden.
2. Cut garlic clove in half and rub over warm toast; brush toast with olive oil and serve at once with soup.
Serves 2.

Variation 1: After rubbing toast with garlic and olive oil, sprinkle 1 tablespoon grated Parmesan cheese over each slice.

Variation 2: Chop and combine 2 unpeeled tomatoes and 2 inner celery stalks. Place on toast after rubbing with garlic and olive oil.

BROTH WITH VEGETABLES

3 cups chicken broth
4 unpeeled small zucchini
1 unpeeled carrot
1 inner celery stalk
Freshly ground black pepper
2 slices coarse white bread
1/2 cup grated Parmesan cheese

1. Place broth in a saucepan, bring to boil, and cook over high heat for 2 minutes.
2. Lower heat to simmer. With a chef's knife, chop vegetables coarsely, add to broth, and cook for 5 minutes; season to taste with pepper.
3. Toast bread and place 1 slice in each soup bowl. Sprinkle each slice with 1 tablespoon grated cheese.
4. Ladle soup over toast and serve hot with remaining grated cheese at table.
Serves 2.

FRESH PEA SOUP

3 cups chicken broth
4 unpeeled small carrots
4 lettuce leaves
2 parsley sprigs (no stems)
1 cup fresh shelled peas, or 1/2 package (about 5 ounces) frozen peas
Freshly ground black pepper

1. Place broth in a saucepan and bring to boil over high heat.
2. Lower heat to simmer. Slice carrots into broth and add lettuce leaves, parsley, and peas. Cook for 7–8 minutes until peas and carrots are tender.
3. Purée soup coarsely in a blender; season to taste with pepper. Serve hot or at room temperature.
Serves 2.

Serve with crusty bread and cheese.

Note: Save large outer leaves of lettuce for adding to soups and vegetable dishes.

PUMPKIN SOUP

In Bologna, the pumpkin is made into soups, filling for tortelloni, and a vegetable pudding; the color is bright, like the autumn leaves.

2 cups chicken broth
1 cup canned pumpkin purée
1/4 cup pastina (tiny soup pasta)
1/2 teaspoon dried thyme
Freshly ground black pepper
Grated Parmesan cheese

1. Combine broth and pumpkin purée in a saucepan; stirring, bring to boil over high heat.
2. Lower heat and add pastina; simmer for 5 minutes.
3. Stir thyme into soup and season to taste with pepper. Simmer for 3 minutes.
4. Serve hot with a bowl of grated cheese at table.
Serves 2.

Variation: Grate 2 unpeeled carrots into pan with broth and pumpkin purée. Bring to boil over high heat and continue as directed.

SPINACH SOUP WITH CORNMEAL

The winter fog in Venice is damp and moist; it casts a dark-gray shadow over the city. Before Easter, the somber city comes alive and is brightened with the Carnevale, pre-Lenten parades, and spectacular fireworks.

The Venetians use cornmeal to make polenta, soup, bread, and a sweet cake.

3 cups chicken or beef broth
1 bunch tender spinach, or 1/2 package
   (about 5 ounces) frozen spinach
1/4 cup yellow cornmeal
2 slices coarse white bread
1/2 cup grated Parmesan cheese

1. Place broth in a saucepan and bring to boil over high heat.
2. Before untying bunch, wash spinach leaves under cold running water; cut stems from spinach and chop leaves coarsely.
3. Lower heat to simmer, place spinach in broth, and cook for 2 minutes.
4. Add cornmeal to broth, 1 tablespoon at a time, stirring until it thickens. Simmer soup for 10 minutes.
5. Toast bread and place 1 slice on bottom of each soup bowl. Sprinkle each slice with 1 tablespoon grated cheese.
6. Ladle soup over toast and serve hot with remaining grated cheese at table. Serves 2.

BROCCOLI SOUP

The cuisine of Milan is very delicate, and totally different from that of the rest of Italy. In warm weather, soup, including thick minestrone, is often served at room temperature or chilled.

3 cups chicken broth
2 stalks broccoli
1 unpeeled ripe tomato
Grated Parmesan cheese

1. Place broth in a saucepan and bring to boil over high heat.
2. Cut off tough stems of broccoli and discard. Lower heat to simmer, slice tender broccoli tops into broth, and cook for 5–6 minutes.
3. Pour broccoli and broth into a blender and coarsely purée.
4. Ladle soup into 2 bowls. With a chef's knife, chop tomato coarsely and place on top of soup.
5. Serve soup at room temperature or chilled with a bowl of grated cheese at table.
Serves 2.

POTATO SOUP

This is a hearty winter soup.

4 cups chicken broth
2–3 medium-size red potatoes
1/2 small yellow onion, or 1 shallot, peeled
6 parsley sprigs (no stems)
Freshly ground black pepper
1/2 cup grated Gruyère cheese

1. Place broth in a saucepan and bring to boil over high heat.
2. Lower heat to simmer. Peel potatoes and slice into broth; add onion and parsley and cook for 7–8 minutes until potatoes are tender. Season to taste with pepper.
3. Purée soup in a blender until smooth. Stir in cheese and serve hot.
Serves 2.

PASTA comes in a hundred different sizes, shapes, and forms, fresh and dried. Pasta can be served in a hundred different ways, rich or plain, hot or cold, combined with fish, meat, vegetables, or cheese. The north favors the flat ribbon-type pasta made with eggs and served with subtly flavored sauces; in the south dried tubular pastas are served with highly seasoned, "angry" sauces. With light, thin pastas like spaghetti and linguine, stick to light sauces; thick pastas like lasagne and penne need a heavier sauce that will coat the pasta and catch in the holes and hollows. Many classic Italian delights such as gnocchi made with ricotta, polenta with cheese, and rice dishes (risotto) fall into the pasta category as well.

A fine pasta dish can be simply made in minutes by tossing cooked pasta in good olive oil, adding grated cheese and crushed black pepper; with a salad and fruit, you have a satisfying meal.

large shell

spaghetti

lasagne

fettuccine

HOW TO COOK PASTA

There is no mystique about cooking pasta. All you need is a large pot with plenty of boiling water: about 3 quarts of water for 1/2 pound of pasta and 6 quarts of water for 1 pound of pasta. Bring the water to a full rolling boil; don't let the water stop boiling when you add the pasta. Add a small amount of pasta at a time, untangling fresh pasta before placing in the water so it doesn't clump. Stir the pasta into the water with a long-handled wooden fork or spoon as you add it, and keep the water boiling hard as the pasta cooks.

The cooking time varies according to whether the pasta is freshly made or dried, thick or thin. Lift out a strand occasionally as the pasta begins to soften and taste for doneness. Fresh pasta takes very little cooking time, about 2–4 minutes, and dried pasta about 5–8 minutes. You must test by tasting to be sure the pasta is al dente—just tender to the bite. There is nothing worse than pasta that is gummy from overcooking.

Drain the pasta immediately into a large strainer or colander placed in the sink; have the sauce ready. Pour the well-drained pasta into a warm bowl and mix quickly with the sauce to coat all the strands. Add freshly grated cheese and serve *immediately.*

Pasta cannot be prepared in advance unless it is for an oven dish. *Never* cook the pasta until you are ready to sit down to eat.

PASTA WITH EGGPLANT SAUCE

Near the famous Villa San Michele in Anacapri a rustic restaurant sits in a lemon grove. The fragrant scent of lemons fills the warm night air; there is a special liqueur made with lemons from the trees. Eggplant is cooked in many wonderful ways.

2 tablespoons olive oil
1/2 teaspoon dried oregano
3 unpeeled ripe tomatoes, or 3 canned
   Italian plum tomatoes, drained
1 unpeeled small eggplant (about 3
   cups chopped)
Crushed red pepper
1 cup penne (short, tubular pasta)
6 parsley sprigs (no stems)
1/2 cup grated Parmesan cheese

1. Fill a large saucepan with water and place over high heat to boil for pasta.
2. Heat oil in a sauté pan over medium heat, add oregano, and stir a few seconds to flavor oil.
3. Slice tomatoes into pan and cook for 3–4 minutes, mashing them with a spoon as they cook.
4. With a chef's knife, chop eggplant coarsely. Stir into pan and season to taste with red pepper. Cover pan and cook for 8–10 minutes.
5. Add pasta to rapidly boiling water and cook until barely tender; drain into a colander and place in a warm bowl.
6. Pour eggplant sauce over hot pasta. Chop parsley and add to bowl; toss carefully with 1/4 cup grated cheese. Serve hot with remaining grated cheese at table.
Serves 2.

PASTA WITH FRESH TOMATOES

This simple dish is made with chopped parsley, black olives, and raw tomatoes stirred into hot pasta at the last minute.

1/2 pound thin vermicelli (extra-thin spaghetti)
3 unpeeled ripe tomatoes
1/4 cup olive oil
2 parsley or basil sprigs (no stems)
8 large black olives, pitted

1. Fill a large saucepan with water and bring to boil over high heat. Add pasta and cook until barely tender.
2. Cut tomatoes into small chunks into a bowl, catching all the juice; add olive oil. Chop parsley and olives and add to bowl.
3. Drain pasta into a colander and place in a bowl. Pour sauce over pasta and toss carefully to mix well. Serve at room temperature.
Serves 2.

PASTA WITH BROCCOLI

1 bunch broccoli
1/4 cup olive oil
2 garlic cloves, peeled
6 anchovy fillets
1/2 cup chicken broth
1 cup small shell pasta
Freshly ground black pepper

1. Fill a large saucepan with water and place over high heat to boil for pasta.
2. With a chef's knife, coarsely chop heads and 1–2 inches of tender stems of broccoli.
3. Heat oil in a sauté pan, add broccoli, and sauté for 1 minute. Chop garlic, stir into pan, and cook for 2 minutes.
4. Add anchovies and broth to pan; cook until broccoli is tender, about 3 minutes.
5. Add pasta shells to rapidly boiling water and cook until barely tender; drain into a colander and place in a warm bowl.
6. Pour broccoli sauce over hot pasta, season to taste with pepper, and toss carefully to mix well. Serve hot.
Serves 2.

PENNE WITH ZUCCHINI

Riding the funicular uphill to Capri there were sunburned patches of vineyard, old stone houses, and a distant view of the sea. In a small restaurant we were greeted by the owner, who recited a litany of pasta dishes combined with fresh vegetables. As a hot starter we had breaded mozzarella rolled in herbs and sautéed in oil; we were served mounds of homemade pasta, and slices of grilled swordfish.

1 cup penne (short, tubular pasta)
3 unpeeled medium-size firm zucchini
1 tablespoon olive oil
Crushed red pepper
1/4 cup grated Parmesan cheese

1. Fill a large saucepan with water and bring to boil over high heat. Add penne and cook until barely tender.
2. Grate zucchini into a sauté pan; stir over high heat 3 minutes. Add oil and season to taste with red pepper; cook, stirring, for 1 minute.
3. Drain pasta into a colander and place in a warm bowl. Pour zucchini and all liquid from pan over pasta. Add grated cheese and toss carefully to mix well. Serve hot.
Serves 2.

PENNE WITH COGNAC SAUCE

In late summer we drove to a coastal fishing village; we ate on the terrace high above the port. The view was framed with flowering vines and palm trees. The meal started with fresh fennel and small artichokes; we had pasta, baked sea bass, and the clear white wine of the nearby vineyards.

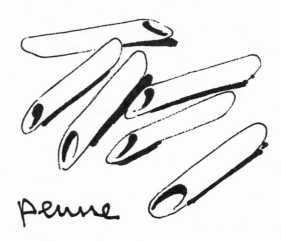

penne

1 cup penne (short, tubular pasta)
1 cup heavy cream
1 tablespoon cognac
1 tablespoon dry white vermouth
1/4 cup grated Parmesan cheese
Freshly ground black pepper

1. Fill a large saucepan with water and bring to boil over high heat. Add penne and cook until barely tender.
2. Pour cream into a saucepan and bring to boil over high heat. Cook, stirring, to reduce and thicken cream, about 2–3 minutes.
3. Add cognac and vermouth to cream and simmer for 2 minutes.
4. Drain penne into a colander and place in a warm bowl. Pour sauce over hot pasta, add grated cheese, and toss carefully to mix well.
5. Season to taste with pepper and serve hot.
Serves 2.

PASTA WITH TUNA SAUCE

In Naples I saw markets with stalls of bright-red peppers, ripe tomatoes, tawny autumn flowers, pyramids of pecorino and mozzarella cheeses, breads studded with citrus fruits or olives. Pasta usually has a fishy flavor, as the south loves clam, sardine, and tuna sauces.

The ingredients for this pasta dish can be kept on the shelf for a spur-of-the-moment meal.

2 tablespoons olive oil
1/2 teaspoon dried oregano
2 unpeeled medium-size ripe tomatoes, or 2 canned Italian plum tomatoes, drained
One 7-ounce can solid light tuna, packed in olive oil (preferably imported Italian tuna), drained
1/2 teaspoon crushed red pepper
1 cup large pasta shells
6 parsley sprigs (no stems)

1. Fill a large saucepan with water and place over high heat to boil for pasta.
2. Heat oil in a sauté pan over medium heat, add oregano, and stir a few seconds to flavor oil.
3. Slice tomatoes into pan and cook for 3–4 minutes until soft, mashing them with a spoon as they cook to make a thick sauce.
4. Stir drained tuna and red pepper into pan and simmer for 6 minutes.
5. Add pasta to rapidly boiling water and cook until barely tender; drain into a colander and place in a warm bowl.
6. Pour tuna sauce over hot pasta. Chop parsley, add to pasta, and toss carefully to mix well. Serve hot.
Serves 2.

PASTA WITH SAFFRON AND CRAB

2 tablespoons dry white vermouth
1/4 teaspoon powdered saffron
1 shallot, peeled
1 cup dry white wine
1 tablespoon dried basil
1 cup heavy cream
1/4 pound fresh or canned crab meat
Freshly ground black pepper
1/2 pound fettuccine

1. Fill a large saucepan with water and place over high heat to boil for pasta.
2. In a small bowl combine vermouth and saffron.
3. Chop shallot and place in a saucepan with wine and basil; bring to boil and cook for 2 minutes. Add cream and cook, stirring, to reduce and thicken sauce, about 5 minutes.
4. Stir saffron mixture into pan, add crab meat, and simmer for 2 minutes over low heat. Season to taste with pepper.
5. Add fettuccine to rapidly boiling water and cook until barely tender; drain into a colander and place in a warm bowl.
6. Pour sauce over hot pasta and toss carefully to mix well. Serve hot.
Serves 2.

SPAGHETTI WITH MUSHROOM AND OLIVE SAUCE

The summer is hot in Sicily: Taormina is a village overlooking the Mediterranean with picturesque streets and Greek ruins, and summer castles for escape from the terrible heat of July and August. This summer pasta dish is meant to be garnished with fresh watercress or mint.

6 unpeeled fresh small white
   mushrooms
10 fresh mint leaves, or 6 parsley sprigs
   (no stems)
10 black olives, pitted
1/4 cup olive oil
2 oranges
1/2 pound thin vermicelli (extra-thin
   spaghetti)
10 black olives, pitted, for garnish
Watercress, for garnish

1. Fill a large saucepan with water and place over high heat to boil for pasta.
2. With a chef's knife, chop mushrooms, mint, and 10 olives.
3. Heat oil in a sauté pan over medium heat, add mushrooms, mint, and olives, and cook together, stirring, for 3 minutes.
4. Squeeze juice of oranges into pan and cook for 1 minute; stir sauce and remove to a large bowl. Grate rind of 1 orange into bowl.
5. Add pasta to rapidly boiling water and cook until barely tender; drain into a colander and place in bowl with sauce.
6. Add 10 whole olives and toss carefully to mix well. Garnish with watercress and serve at room temperature.
Serves 2.

PASTA WITH GORGONZOLA AND BASIL

In a small restaurant in Milan I was served a plate with a colorful trilogy: pasta with gorgonzola, pasta with zucchini, and risotto with shrimp sauce—the invention of an imaginative chef.

1 cup heavy cream
1/4 pound gorgonzola cheese
2 tablespoons dry white wine
1/2 pound green tagliarini (ribbon noodles)
2 tablespoons pine nuts
10 fresh basil leaves (optional)
Freshly ground black pepper

1. Fill a large saucepan with water and place over high heat to boil for pasta.
2. Pour cream into a saucepan and bring to boil over high heat. Cook, stirring, to reduce and thicken cream, about 2–3 minutes.
3. Lower heat; stir cheese into cream. Add wine and cook until cheese melts and sauce is well mixed, about 2 minutes.
4. Add pasta to rapidly boiling water and cook until barely tender; drain into a colander and place in a warm bowl.
5. Pour sauce over hot pasta. Add pine nuts, basil leaves, and pepper to taste and toss carefully to mix well.
Serve hot.
Serves 2.

GREEN AND WHITE PASTA
(STRAW AND HAY)

Wherever you go in Tuscany, in the valleys or hills, you will find the colors and landscapes that inspired the backgrounds of Renaissance paintings and tapestries: wood-covered hills, castles and red-tile-roofed villages, clusters of pines, dark rivers, and deep-green cypress trees.

In northern Italy this dish is called straw and hay.

1 tablespoon unsalted butter
4 thin slices prosciutto
1/2 cup dry white wine
1/2 cup heavy cream
Freshly ground black pepper
1/4 pound white fettuccine
1/4 pound green fettuccine
1/4 cup grated Parmesan cheese

1. Fill a large saucepan with water and place over high heat to boil for pasta.
2. Melt butter in a sauté pan over medium heat. Cut prosciutto into long, thin strips, stir into pan, and sauté for 2 minutes.
3. Add wine to pan and boil for 2 minutes. Stir in cream and cook for 2 minutes; season to taste with pepper.
4. Add white and green fettuccine to rapidly boiling water and cook until barely tender; drain into a colander and place in a warm bowl.
5. Pour sauce over hot pasta, add cheese, and toss carefully to mix well. Serve hot.
Serves 2.

QUICKLY MADE SAUCES

All of these sauces are made with raw ingredients in just seconds.

● *Chopped Olives in Oil:* Coarsely purée in a blender 10 black olives (pitted), 2 tablespoons olive oil, and 2 parsley sprigs (no stems). Stir into hot pasta, or use to sauté meat, fish, or poultry.

● *Herbs in Oil:* Combine 1 tablespoon dried oregano or thyme and 2 tablespoons olive oil in a bowl; mix well. Stir into hot pasta, or use to sauté meat, fish, or poultry.

● *Tomatoes in Oil:* Coarsely purée in a blender 1 unpeeled ripe tomato, 1/2 shallot (peeled), 1 garlic clove (peeled), 2 parsley sprigs (no stems), and 2 tablespoons olive oil. Stir into hot pasta or into fish or vegetable soups, use as a sauce for fish, meat, or vegetables, or simply eat with crusty bread.

● *Ricotta Cheese Sauce:* Combine in a blender 1/2 cup ricotta cheese, 2 tablespoons heavy cream, and 1/2 teaspoon *each* dried thyme and oregano; season to taste with freshly ground black pepper. Stir into hot pasta, or eat with crusty bread.

RICE

Rice is an essential part of the daily meal in northern Italy. The Italian method of cooking rice leaves each grain separate and slightly resistant to the teeth, totally different from the rice dishes of other countries. Italian rice is a must for cooking risotto, as other rice does not absorb broth in the same way. You can find Italian Arborio rice in Italian markets and some supermakets.

It is the creaminess that gives risotto its unique flavor and character; this is achieved by the combination of butter, broth, and quantities of freshly grated cheese used with the rice. The secret of cooking a good risotto is simple: the rice is sautéed in butter, a small amount of hot broth is added slowly, and only when the rice has absorbed all of the previous liquid is more added; the rice should just barely be covered with broth; the cheese is stirred in at the finish. Whatever fish, meat, or vegetables go with the rice are cooked into it, making risotto a complete meal.

Remember:
- Do not wash Italian rice.
- Always use *hot* broth.
- Always use *freshly* grated cheese.
- The only way to test doneness is to bite into a grain of rice; it should be firm, but not hard.

RISOTTO WITH FONTINA

The cheese for this satisfying dish must be imported Italian fontina, as it melts beautifully and gives a lovely smooth texture to the risotto.

3 cups chicken broth
1 tablespoon unsalted butter
1/2 cup Italian Arborio rice
2 unpeeled small carrots
1/2 cup grated fontina or Parmesan
  cheese

1. Place broth in a saucepan and simmer over low heat.
2. Melt butter in a sauté pan over medium heat; add rice and stir with a wooden spoon until each grain of rice is shiny and glazed, about 2 minutes. Pour 1/2 cup hot broth into pan; stir and cook slowly for 3–4 minutes until broth is absorbed.
3. Grate carrots and stir into rice. Continue adding broth, 1/2 cup at a time, as liquid is absorbed.
4. After 10–12 minutes, taste the rice as it should be done. Stir grated cheese into rice so mixture blends into a creamy consistency. Serve immediately. Serves 2.

Note: The exact amount of broth needed to cook risotto can never be specified; you may not use it all or you may need a little more. The amount of liquid used varies with the type of rice, so continue to add broth only until the rice is tender.

RISOTTO WITH PINK SHRIMP SAUCE

Milan, most contemporary of Italian cities, is a business and banking center. This is a city of understated elegance, where you must look beyond the facades. When a heavy door opens, there are secret gardens and courtyards with small restaurants to be discovered.

3 cups chicken broth
1/2 pound raw shrimp, cleaned
1 unpeeled small ripe tomato
1 tablespoon unsalted butter
1/2 cup Italian Arborio rice
1/2 cup dry white wine

1. Place broth in a saucepan and simmer over low heat.
2. Put shrimp, tomato, and 1 cup broth in a blender and purée coarsely.
3. Melt butter in a sauté pan over medium heat; add rice and stir with a wooden spoon until each grain of rice is shiny and glazed, about 2 minutes. Pour 1/2 cup hot broth into pan; stir and cook slowly for 3–4 minutes until broth is absorbed.
4. Stir shrimp purée into rice. Add wine and stir. When wine is absorbed, continue adding broth, 1/2 cup at a time, as liquid is absorbed.
5. After 10–12 minutes, taste the rice as it should be done. Serve immediately. Serves 2.

When rice is combined with fish, grated cheese is not served.

RISOTTO WITH ASPARAGUS

3 cups chicken broth
2 tablespoons unsalted butter
1/2 cup Italian Arborio rice
8 fresh or frozen asparagus spears
Freshly ground black pepper
1/2 cup grated Parmesan cheese

1. Place broth in a saucepan and simmer over low heat.
2. Melt butter in a sauté pan over medium heat; add rice and stir with a wooden spoon until each grain of rice is shiny and glazed, about 2 minutes. Pour 1/2 cup hot broth into pan; stir and cook slowly for 3–4 minutes until broth is absorbed.
3. Cut off and discard tough ends of asparagus. Cut tips and tender stems crosswise into thin slices; stir into rice.
4. Continue adding broth, 1/2 cup at a time, as liquid is absorbed. Season to taste with pepper.
5. After 10–12 minutes, taste the rice as it should be done. Stir grated cheese into rice so mixture blends into a creamy consistency. Serve immediately. Serves 2.

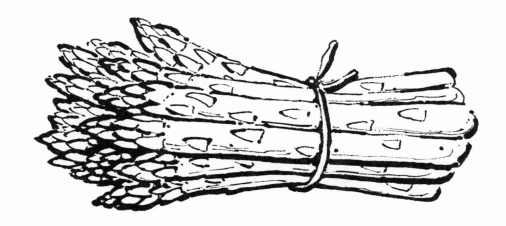

RISOTTO WITH VEGETABLES

May in Florence is a time of concerts, opera, and ballet. *Risotto primavera* is given its name because of the mixture of spring vegetables.

3 cups chicken broth
1 tablespoon unsalted butter
1/2 cup Italian Arborio rice
1/2 cup dry white wine
2 unpeeled small carrots
2 unpeeled small zucchini
4 unpeeled fresh white mushrooms
Handful of shelled peas
Freshly ground black pepper
1/4 cup grated Parmesan cheese

1. Place broth in a saucepan and simmer over low heat.
2. Melt butter in a sauté pan over medium heat; add rice and stir with a wooden spoon until each grain of rice is shiny and glazed, about 2 minutes. Pour 1/2 cup hot broth into pan; stir and cook slowly for 3–4 minutes until broth is absorbed.
3. Stir wine into rice and cook until absorbed.
4. Grate carrots and zucchini; with a chef's knife, chop mushrooms coarsely. Stir vegetables, including peas, into pan.
5. Continue adding broth, 1/2 cup at a time, as liquid is absorbed. Season to taste with pepper.
6. After 10–12 minutes, taste the rice as it should be done. Stir grated cheese into rice so mixture blends into a creamy consistency. Serve immediately. Serves 2.

POLENTA

Polenta, yellow cornmeal, is very important to the northern Italians; for many in Lombardy and around Venice, it replaces bread.

Polenta must be cooked in boiling water until very thick; it is then served with butter and cheese or with a sauce of meat, codfish, mushrooms, sausages, tomatoes, ham, or tiny birds. One of the signs of well-cooked polenta is the crusty crust that clings to the sides of the pan when it is done. Cold polenta may be sliced and fried in butter; as a child I loved slices of hot and crisp polenta with jelly for breakfast.

Available in coarse and fine grinds, polenta can be found in Italian markets, often in bulk. The coarse grind needs more water for cooking than the fine grind.

POLENTA WITH CHEESE

3 cups water
1 cup coarse yellow cornmeal
1 tablespoon unsalted butter, at room temperature
1/2 cup grated fontina or Swiss cheese (should be a cheese that melts easily), at room temperature

1. Put water in a heavy saucepan and bring to boil over high heat.
2. Pour cornmeal slowly into boiling water, stirring with a long-handled wooden spoon to keep cornmeal smooth as it thickens.
3. Reduce heat to low and allow cornmeal to cook slowly for 15–20 minutes until a crust forms around the sides of the pan.
4. Stir in butter and grated cheese. The polenta should be a smooth mixture.
Serve hot.
Serves 2.

Variation: Add 1/2 teaspoon powdered saffron to boiling water before adding cornmeal.

RICOTTA GNOCCHI

Try these delicate gnocchi; they are as light as air, and take only seconds to make. Serve them with a vegetable for your meal.

1/2 cup ricotta cheese
3 tablespoons all-purpose flour
1 egg yolk
1/4 cup grated Parmesan cheese
2 tablespoons unsalted butter

Preheat oven to 350°F
1. Fill a large saucepan with water and place over high heat to boil for gnocchi.
2. In a bowl combine ricotta, 1 table-spoon flour, egg yolk, and 2 tablespoons grated cheese; mix well with a tablespoon.
3. Put 2 tablespoons flour on a paper towel, place ricotta mixture in flour, and form into a large ball by rolling in flour.
4. Take pieces of ricotta dough with your fingers and form into small ovals, making about 20 gnocchi. If sticky, roll ovals in flour.
5. Lower heat under boiling water, add 6–7 gnocchi to simmering water, and poach about 1 minute, or until they rise to the surface. Remove gnocchi from water with a slotted spoon and place in an oven dish. Repeat until all are cooked.
6. Dot gnocchi with bits of butter and sprinkle with 2 tablespoons grated cheese. Place in *preheated* oven for about 2 minutes until butter and cheese are melted. Serve hot.
Serves 2.

SEMOLINA GNOCCHI

Rome has good modest restaurants in all areas, piazzas with flowing fountains, towering columns, great monuments, monasteries, and churches with frescoes. There are so many grand houses and gardens it would take a lifetime to explore them all.

This dish from Rome makes a fast and nourishing meal. Semolina is a light-yellow flour; it can be found in Italian markets, in packages or bulk.

1 cup milk
1/2 cup semolina
2 tablespoons unsalted butter, at room
   temperature
1 egg
3/4 cup grated Parmesan cheese

Preheat oven to 400°F
1. Put milk in a saucepan and bring to boil over medium heat.
2. Lower heat to simmer and add semolina slowly, stirring with a wooden spoon to keep semolina smooth.
3. Cook over medium-low heat, stirring as semolina thickens, about 2 minutes.
4. Remove pan from heat and stir butter into semolina.
5. Break egg into a bowl, blend with a whisk, and mix in 1/2 cup grated cheese.
6. Stir egg mixture into semolina with a spoon, beating well. Put semolina into a buttered 6 X 9-inch oven dish; spread evenly with the back of a tablespoon.
7. Sprinkle 1/4 cup grated cheese over top and place in *preheated* oven about 5 minutes until golden. Serve hot.
Serves 2.

FISH is cooked quickly and easily by the Italians, usually in a sauté pan, to retain the fresh flavor of the sea. Parsley, garlic, capers, anchovies, fennel, and olives are favorite seasonings, and lemon is always used as a garnish.

The sea supplies Italy with a large variety of fish, as the country is surrounded by water on three sides. In Naples during the sardine season, a purée of sardines, pine nuts, and the green leaves of wild fennel is tossed with thin spaghetti. On Capri, the pasta is served with a tuna sauce; in Venice, fish is melted in soup, and a mix of fish may be steamed in a paper bag.

One bright early morning on Capri I watched the fishermen unload baskets of bright fish from boats. The fish market on the main piazza has a spotless white tile floor, marble counters and tables. Small plump fish lay by the sink; shellfish waited in seaweed-lined baskets for delivery to the local restaurants. Customers selected fish from the glistening pile laid out on green sea fronds by the door.

The fish of other countries always look exotic to me—sea urchins, mussels, squid, oysters; some are round with silver bodies, some long with savage jaws or tentacles, some like giant open flowers. In our polluted times, fish is becoming scarce everywhere, and more expensive. It is important to cook it properly to retain its goodness.

Remember:
- When buying fish, allow 1/4 pound per person.
- Rub the fish with lemon juice before you bake, broil, or poach it. Lemon will lend flavor, helps prevent it from breaking, and preserves color.
- To test for freshness, press fish with your finger. If the flesh springs back, the fish is fresh; if a dent remains, it is not.
- To test for doneness, insert the tines of a fork into the thickest part of the fish; if it flakes easily it is done.

SEA BASS WITH PRAWNS

2 sea bass fillets (about 1/2 pound)
3 unpeeled fresh white mushrooms
1/4 pound prawns, cleaned (leave tails on)
1/4 cup heavy cream
1/4 cup dry white vermouth
1/4 cup grated Parmesan cheese
Paprika
1 lemon

Preheat oven to 375°F
1. Place fillets in an oven dish. Slice mushrooms over fish, and arrange prawns around fillets.
2. Combine cream and vermouth and pour over fish. Sprinkle cheese over fish and season to taste with paprika.
3. Place dish in *preheated* oven and bake about 10 minutes until fish flakes when tested with a fork and sauce is browned on top.
4. Serve fish hot with sauce from dish; garnish with lemon.
Serves 2.

FILLETS OF SOLE MARSALA

2 tablespoons unsalted butter
2 thin sole fillets
1/4 cup Marsala wine
2 tablespoons heavy cream
1 lemon

1. Heat butter to foaming in a sauté pan, add sole fillets, and cook until lightly golden, about 1 minute on each side. Pour out butter.
2. Combine Marsala and cream, pour into pan, and cook, stirring, for 3 minutes.
3. Serve fish hot with sauce from pan; garnish with lemon.
Serves 2.

FILLETS OF SOLE WITH CAPERS

1 tablespoon unsalted butter
2 thin sole fillets
1/4 cup dry white wine
2 tablespoons capers, drained
1 lemon
Freshly ground black pepper
4 parsley sprigs (no stems)

1. Heat butter to foaming in a sauté pan, add sole fillets, and cook until golden brown, about 2 minutes on each side. Remove fish to a warm plate.
2. Pour wine into pan, and stir bottom of pan to scrape cooked bits into sauce. Add capers and squeeze in juice of lemon; season to taste with pepper.
3. Bring sauce to boil over high heat and cook for 2 minutes.
4. Pour sauce over fish. Chop parsley and sprinkle on top. Serve hot.
Serves 2.

Fennel with Oil and Lemon is good with this dish.

SCALLOPS WITH PARSLEY SAUCE

On the island of Elba there is an old stone path up the mountain to a monastery filled with legends of Napoleon; I saw hills and fields swept with vineyards, beautiful bays, and turquoise water. The fish and game are always fresh; the vegetables, peaches, and tomatoes are luscious; the local cheese is creamy. There are *biscotti,* hard almond cookies, to dip in sweet wine at the end of a meal.

1/4 cup olive oil
12 parsley sprigs (no stems)
2 garlic cloves, or 1 shallot, peeled
2 lemons
1/2 pound scallops
Watercress

Preheat oven to 400°F
1. Place oil, parsley, and garlic in a blender and purée; squeeze in juice of 1 lemon.
2. Cut scallops in half if large. Place the scallops in an oven dish and pour parsley sauce over them.
3. Place dish in *preheated* oven and cook until scallops are golden brown on both sides, about 5 minutes. Turn scallops once while cooking and baste with sauce. Do not overcook.
4. Serve scallops hot; garnish with watercress and lemon.
Serves 2.

Note: Prawns, too, can be cooked with this sauce.

POACHED HALIBUT
WITH CAPER SAUCE

A two-hour drive from Milan, Portofino is almost inaccessible on a mountain peninsula, and so is best reached by boat. You can watch small fishing boats bringing in the day's catch from Santa Margherita, a nearby neighbor. There is plenty of fish and shellfish; sea bass is baked with olives, ravioli are served in a walnut sauce, and halibut is sauced with capers.

2 cups water
1/2 cup dry white wine
1 onion
4 parsley sprigs
1 bay leaf
1/2 pound halibut, sea bass, or any firm
   white fish, boned and skinned
Caper Sauce (following), or Red Sauce
   (page 89)

1. Combine water and wine in a saucepan and bring to boil. Lower heat to simmer, and slice onion into pan; add parsley and bay leaf.
2. Place fish in water and simmer gently for 6–8 minutes, or until fish flakes when tested with a fork.
3. Remove fish from water and arrange on a plate. Serve at room temperature with Caper Sauce.
Serves 2.

CAPER SAUCE

10 parsley sprigs (no stems)
1/2 cup pine nuts or walnuts
1/4 cup capers, drained
2 tablespoons red wine vinegar
1 slice fresh white bread, crust removed
1/2 cup olive oil

1. Place parsley, pine nuts, capers, vinegar, and bread in a blender to purée.
2. With motor running, slowly add oil in a thin stream; blend until well mixed.
Makes about 1 cup.

This sauce is also good with raw or cooked vegetables, or endive.

BROILED FISH ON SKEWERS

1/2 pound halibut, swordfish, red
  snapper, or any firm white fish, boned
  and skinned
1/4 cup olive oil
1/4 cup dry white vermouth
2 lemons
1 small onion
8 parsley sprigs (no stems)
Freshly ground black pepper

Preheat broiler at full broil
1. Cut fish into 2-inch squares and
place in a bowl.
2. Pour olive oil and vermouth into bowl
and squeeze in juice of 1 lemon; gently
turn fish in sauce to cover all sides.
3. Cut onion into pieces. Thread fish
squares, parsley sprigs, and onion pieces
alternately on thin wooden skewers.
Place skewers on an oven sheet and
season to taste with pepper.
4. Place fish under *preheated* broiler
and cook about 7 minutes, or until fish
flakes when tested with a fork; turn
often and baste with sauce in bowl.
5. Serve fish hot; garnish with lemon.
Serves 2.

BAKED FISH WITH TOMATOES

On Capri, there are long walks above
the sea through pines and paths bordered
with cactus; below are bright-colored
rocks along the coast. I Faraglioni,
three rocks that jut out of the water,
change color as the sun shifts. Natives
have small boats to fish, and swim away
from the rocky shore.

1/2 pound cod, swordfish, or halibut,
   boned and skinned
2 unpeeled ripe tomatoes, or 2 canned
   Italian plum tomatoes, drained
1/2 sweet red pepper
2 tablespoons olive oil
1/2 teaspoon dried oregano
1/4 cup green olives, pitted
1/2 cup dry white wine

Preheat oven to 400°F
1. Place fish in an oven dish; slice
tomatoes and red pepper into dish
around fish.
2. Pour oil over fish and vegetables;
sprinkle with oregano and olives.
3. Place dish in *preheated* oven for 10
minutes. Remove from oven, pour wine
into bottom of dish, and baste fish.
4. Return dish to oven and bake for 5
minutes until fish flakes when tested
with a fork.
5. Serve fish hot with sauce from dish.
Serves 2.

BRAISED SALMON

Two 1-inch-thick center-cut salmon
   steaks
1 tablespoon unsalted butter
2 teaspoons fennel seeds
1 shallot, peeled
3 lettuce leaves
1 cup dry white wine
Sea salt
Freshly ground black pepper

Preheat oven to 375°F
1. Arrange salmon in an oven dish; dot
with butter and sprinkle with fennel
seeds.
2. With a chef's knife, chop shallot and
lettuce coarsely and sprinkle over
salmon.
3. Pour wine into bottom of dish; season
to taste. Cover dish with a piece of
waxed paper; place dish in *preheated*
oven for 10–12 minutes until salmon
flakes when tested with a fork.
4. Serve hot with sauce from dish.
Serves 2.

SALMON COOKED IN VERMOUTH

This is a light and satisfying meal.

2 cups water
1 cup dry white vermouth
1/4 teaspoon dried thyme
1/2 pound salmon, boned and skinned
1 lemon
1 small avocado
1 unpeeled cucumber
Orange Mayonnaise (page 125)

1. Combine water and vermouth in a
saucepan and bring to a boil over high
heat. Lower heat and add thyme.
2. Place salmon in water and simmer
gently for 6–8 minutes, or until fish
flakes when tested with a fork.
3. Remove fish from water and arrange
on a plate. Slice lemon, avocado, and
cucumber thinly onto plate with salmon.
Serve at room temperature with Orange
Mayonnaise (or crème fraîche; homemade, page 23).
Serves 2.

Note: Prawns or a piece of sea bass or
halibut can be poached in this broth.

VENETIAN FISH SOUP

The traditional Italian meal on Christmas Eve usually consists of fish, as it is a day of fasting; an elaborate feast is served on Christmas Day. One Christmas Eve we celebrated mass in the cathedral in Venice, a spectacular scene with hundreds of candles and a large choir, the bishop wearing gold-and-white vestments and red-satin slippers.

1/4 cup olive oil
1 garlic clove, peeled
2 small slices coarse white bread
1/2 pound sea bass or red snapper, skinned and boned
4 parsley sprigs (no stems)
1/4 teaspoon dried oregano
2 unpeeled ripe tomatoes, or 2 canned Italian plum tomatoes, drained
1/2 cup dry white wine
1/4 teaspoon powdered saffron
2 cups bottled clam juice or water

1. Heat oil in a sauté pan over medium heat, add garlic, and stir a few seconds to flavor oil.
2. Put bread slices in pan and cook until crisp and golden on both sides. Discard garlic and place fried bread in soup bowls.
3. Place fish in pan and cook until lightly golden on both sides; pour out oil.
4. Chop parsley and stir into pan with oregano; slice tomatoes into pan.
5. Combine wine, saffron, and clam juice, stirring to mix well; pour into pan. Bring soup to boil, lower heat, and cook over medium heat for 10–15 minutes until fish flakes when tested with a fork.
6. Ladle hot soup over fried bread in bowls. Serve hot.
Serves 2.

SHRIMP FLORENTINE

In September there is a traditional festival: carts, and crowds carrying colored paper lanterns parade through Florence; there is dancing and music in the streets, and local songs are sung.

2 tablespoons olive oil
1/2 pound raw shrimp, cleaned
1 garlic clove, peeled
1 unpeeled small ripe tomato
1 lemon
4 parsley sprigs (no stems)

1. Heat oil in a sauté pan over medium heat and add shrimp and garlic; sauté, stirring, for 2 minutes.
2. Slice tomato into pan and squeeze in juice of lemon; simmer over low heat for 3 minutes. Discard garlic clove.
3. Chop parsley and sprinkle over shrimp. Serve hot with sauce from pan. Serves 2.

TUNA WITH CARROTS

2 tablespoons olive oil
1/2 teaspoon dried oregano
Two 1-inch-thick tuna fillets (about 1/2 pound)
4 unpeeled small carrots
1/2 small yellow onion
1/2 cup dry white wine
Freshly ground black pepper

1. Heat oil in a sauté pan over medium heat, add oregano, and stir a few seconds to flavor oil.
2. Add tuna to pan and cook for 2 minutes on each side until golden.
3. Slice carrots and onion into pan; stir in wine.
4. Lower heat, cover, and cook for 8–10 minutes until fish flakes when tested with a fork and carrots are tender.
5. Season to taste with pepper. Place tuna and vegetables on a warm plate and serve immediately.
Serves 2.

CRAB LEGS WITH MUSHROOMS

This is a quick meal for one or two, or it can be increased for many.

2 tablespoons unsalted butter
6 unpeeled fresh mushrooms
1 shallot, peeled
2 thin slices prosciutto (optional)
8 crab legs, or 1 cup crab meat (canned crab may be used)
1/2 cup dry white wine
Freshly ground black pepper

1. Melt butter in a sauté pan over medium heat.
2. Chop mushrooms and shallot; cut prosciutto into long, thin strips. Place in pan and cook for 1 minute.
3. Stir crab legs into pan and cook for 1 minute. Pour wine into pan and simmer for 2 minutes; season to taste with pepper.
4. Serve crab legs hot with sauce from pan.
Serves 2.

Serve with peas or Grated Carrots.

CHICKEN (and other fowl) was a luxury in Italy until a few years ago, and was served only on special occasions. Italians have learned to cook fowl in many exquisite and delicate ways, using every precious scrap. They bone the breast, cook it quickly in oil and butter, and combine it with herbs, mushrooms, red peppers, tomatoes, olives, or broth; scraps of chopped chicken are used to fill ravioli and tortellini; large chickens and capons are stuffed with sausages and basted with wine.

The Florentines baste fowl with lemon and oil; they flatten chicken so it is crisp when grilled. In Milan, thinly sliced turkey breast rolled in cheese and bread crumbs and sautéed in butter is a special treat. In Bologna, chicken breast comes with a slice of ham and a layer of cheese on top.

In Trastevere, the area of Rome most unaltered from medieval times, the narrow streets are filled with people, roaring motorcycles, and cars with blaring horns. Live squawking fowl ran freely in this neighborhood not too long ago, when the farmer's wife hand-fed her fowl with good grain. Now large-scale commercial chicken raising is common in Italy, too. It is difficult, but worth it, to find chickens naturally bred because they have superior flavor.

Remember:
- Try to buy small fowl; they are succulent, with firm and supple flesh.
- Remove all yellow fat before cooking, and rub fowl with lemon to accent flavor.
- Never add salt to fowl until the end of cooking, as salt will draw the juices.
- Poach chicken or turkey breasts in gently simmering broth; boiling will toughen them.
- Season with fresh herbs; tarragon, rosemary, and oregano complement poultry, but be careful not to overseason. Place a sprig of thyme on breast as it cooks.
- Prick the flesh with a fork to test for doneness; if the liquid runs clear, it is ready to eat.
- Always save the bones, carcass, skin, and fat to make broth.

HOW TO BONE A CHICKEN BREAST

Place chicken breast flesh side down on a flat surface. Insert the blade of a boning knife under the flesh and, following the bone, cut the meat away, lifting with your fingers. When the flesh is free of the bone, cut the breast in half. Slip the knife under the skin and carefully cut away the skin.

Save all skin, trimmings, and bones for making chicken broth; place in a plastic bag and freeze, if not using immediately.

CHICKEN OR SQUAB
WITH MUSTARD SAUCE

Castel Gandolfo, the Pope's summer
retreat, has beautifully terraced gardens,
cypresses, and oleanders, and rose
trees that grow in formal rows about
the ancient ruins; I love going there in
the late summer for picnics.

1 baby chicken* or squab (about 1
    pound)
2 tablespoons olive or safflower oil
2 teaspoons Dijon mustard
1/4 teaspoon crushed red pepper
2 tablespoons dry white wine or dry
    white vermouth
1 lemon

Preheat oven to 500°F
1. Split and butterfly chicken by running
a sharp boning knife along the back.
Place bird on a wooden board. With the
flat side of a chef's knife, flatten chicken
to a uniform thickness.
2. Mix oil, mustard, red pepper, and
wine in a small bowl; squeeze in juice
of lemon. Place chicken, breast side up,
in an oven dish and brush with sauce.
3. Place chicken in *preheated* oven and
cook about 7 minutes on each side
until tender and golden; baste with
sauce while cooking.
4. Pour sauce from pan over chicken
and serve hot or at room temperature.
Serves 2.

Serve with a green salad on the same
plate, as the hot mustard sauce is also
good on lettuce.

* A baby chicken, called a poussin, is
ideal for 1–2 persons. Available in
specialty poultry markets and some
supermarkets, a poussin weighs about
1-1/4 pounds.

CHICKEN WITH MUSHROOMS

1 tablespoon unsalted butter
1 tablespoon olive oil
3 chicken legs
3 chicken thighs
6 unpeeled fresh white mushrooms
1 shallot, peeled
1/2 cup dry white wine
1/4 teaspoon dried thyme
Freshly ground black pepper
10 parsley sprigs (no stems)

1. Heat butter and oil in a sauté pan over medium heat, add chicken pieces, and brown on all sides, about 5 minutes.
2. Slice mushrooms into pan. Chop shallot, stir into pan, and cook with mushrooms for a few seconds.
3. Pour wine into pan, add thyme, and season to taste with pepper, stirring well.
4. Cover, lower heat, and cook about 10 minutes until chicken is tender.
5. Chop parsley and sprinkle over chicken. Serve hot with sauce from pan. Serves 2.

COUNTRY CHICKEN SAUTE

It is a pleasure to go to the country to see the change of season. Lunch is lovely in a late summer garden of vines and pomegranates, lemon trees, roses, and giant dahlias.

1 whole chicken breast, halved, boned, and skinned
1 tablespoon olive oil
1 tablespoon unsalted butter
1 sweet red pepper (about 1 cup chopped)
1 teaspoon fennel seeds, or 1/2 teaspoon dried oregano
10 black olives, pitted
1/2 cup dry white wine
Freshly ground black pepper

1. Cut each piece of breast in half lengthwise, making 4 strips. Place chicken strips on a wooden board and slap lightly with the flat side of a chef's knife to flatten.
2. Heat oil and butter in a sauté pan over medium heat, add chicken, and cook until golden brown, about 2 minutes on each side.
3. With a chef's knife, chop red pepper coarsely and stir into pan; add fennel seeds and olives.
4. Pour wine into bottom of pan; stir and season to taste with pepper.
5. Cook over medium heat about 10 minutes until chicken is tender.
6. Serve chicken hot with sauce from pan.
Serves 2.

BREAST OF CHICKEN WITH CHOPPED CELERY

This is an easy and adaptable dish for entertaining, as it can be increased from two to ten servings.

1/4 cup grated Parmesan cheese
1 whole chicken breast, halved, boned, and skinned
4 celery stalks
1 cup heavy cream
1 teaspoon dried rosemary
1 teaspoon dried thyme
Paprika

Preheat oven to 450°F
1. Place grated cheese on a piece of waxed paper; coat chicken with cheese on all sides and put in an oven dish.
2. With a chef's knife, chop celery coarsely and arrange around chicken. Pour cream over chicken, sprinkle with herbs, and dust to taste with paprika.
3. Place chicken in *preheated* oven and cook about 15 minutes until golden brown on top.
4. Serve chicken hot with sauce from pan.
Serves 2.

CHICKEN ON SKEWERS

This can be served on a bed of rice or thin pasta.

1 whole chicken breast, boned and skinned
2 chicken thighs, boned and skinned
2 tablespoons unsalted butter
1 lemon
6 unpeeled garlic cloves

Preheat oven to 475°F
1. Cut chicken meat into neat 2-inch squares.
2. Thread chicken onto thin wooden skewers, alternating white and dark meat; put into an oven dish.
3. Melt butter in a pan over low heat; squeeze in juice of lemon and add garlic cloves.
4. Pour sauce over chicken in dish; place in *preheated* oven about 10–12 minutes, basting 2–3 times and turning chicken as it browns.
5. Serve chicken hot with juices from dish poured over.
Serves 2.

CHICKEN WITH ARTICHOKES, ROMAN STYLE

Roman style is always sparing of garlic.

2 tablespoons olive oil
1 garlic clove, peeled
1/2 chicken breast, boned and skinned
3 chicken legs
3 chicken thighs
1 unpeeled ripe tomato
3 artichoke hearts or bottoms (canned or frozen)
1/4 cup chicken broth
1/4 cup sweet red vermouth

1. Heat oil in a sauté pan over medium heat, add garlic, and cook for 1 minute. Discard garlic clove.
2. Cut chicken breast in half lengthwise; add all chicken pieces to pan and cook over medium heat until brown on all sides, about 5 minutes.
3. Slice tomato into pan. Cut artichoke hearts in halves or quarters into pan.
4. Stir broth and vermouth into pan, cover, and cook over low heat about 10 minutes until chicken is tender.
5. Serve chicken hot with sauce from pan.
Serves 2.

SESAME CHICKEN

This is an easy, easy dish.

2 tablespoons unsalted butter
1/8 teaspoon crushed red pepper
6 chicken legs or thighs
1/2 cup grated Parmesan cheese
1/4 cup sesame seeds
1 lemon

Preheat oven to 400°F
1. Melt butter in an oven dish and add red pepper. Dip chicken pieces in butter, coating well; push chicken to side of dish.
2. In same oven dish, mix cheese and sesame seeds. Roll chicken in mixture, coating well.
3. Place chicken in *preheated* oven for 10–15 minutes until crisp and golden.
4. Serve chicken at room temperature; garnish with lemon.
Serves 2.

CHICKEN WINGS, ROMAN STYLE

In August the gardens of the Villa Borghese tremble in the heat; the animals in the zoo are limp and can hardly hold up their heads. Crossing a street wilts you, and not even shadows from the buildings offer relief. Near the Piazza Navona with the Bernini fountains, a small trattoria is dark and cool inside. You can see a mound of ripe fruit on the cart; the black and green figs are plump with sweet red flesh. We had the perfect summer menu: figs with prosciutto, chicken wings, and a tart ice.

1 tablespoon olive oil
1 tablespoon unsalted butter
1/2 teaspoon dried thyme
1/2 pound chicken wings
1 shallot, peeled
2 thin slices prosciutto
1/2 cup dry white wine
2 unpeeled ripe tomatoes
Freshly ground black pepper

1. Heat oil and butter in a sauté pan over medium heat, add thyme, and stir a few seconds.
2. Add chicken wings and sauté until golden brown on all sides, about 4 minutes.
3. Chop shallot and cut prosciutto into long, thin strips; add to pan and sauté with chicken wings for 1 minute.
4. Pour wine into bottom of pan; slice tomatoes into pan and season to taste with pepper, stirring well.
5. Bring to boil, cover, lower heat, and simmer about 10 minutes until the wings are tender.
6. Serve chicken wings hot with sauce from pan.
Serves 2.

CHICKEN LIVERS FLORENTINE

Every year in Florence there is a famous ball game, preceded by a magnificent procession in sixteenth-century costume.

2 tablespoons unsalted butter
2 thin slices coarse white bread
1/2 pound chicken livers
1/2 cup sweet red vermouth or Marsala wine
1/4 teaspoon dried sage
Freshly ground black pepper

1. Melt butter in a sauté pan over medium heat, add bread, and cook on both sides until golden; remove from pan.
2. Stir livers into pan and cook, turning, for 2 minutes.
3. Pour vermouth into pan and add sage; stir bottom of pan to scrape cooked bits into sauce. Season to taste with pepper. Cook over medium heat for 2 minutes.
4. Serve livers hot on sautéed bread; pour sauce from pan over livers.
Serves 2.

TURKEY BREAST
WITH FOIE GRAS SAUCE

Bologna, culinary capital of Italy, is located on the edge of the fertile Po Valley, Italy's main agricultural area; cooking, eating, and drinking are taken seriously here.

1/2 small turkey breast, boned and
   skinned,* or 2 fillets
2 tablespoons unsalted butter
1 cup heavy cream
1 small tin foie gras (the inexpensive
   variety)
Freshly ground black pepper

1. Cut turkey breast into 4 long strips. Place strips on a wooden board and slap lightly with the flat side of a chef's knife to flatten.
2. Heat butter to foaming in a sauté pan, add turkey slices, and cook until golden brown, about 2 minutes on each side.
3. Pour 1/2 cup cream into pan, stirring. Bring to boil over high heat and stir in foie gras.
4. Simmer for 8–10 minutes; add more cream as needed to thin sauce.
5. Season to taste with pepper. Serve turkey hot with sauce from pan.
Serves 2.

*Most small half turkey breasts weigh about 2 pounds boned and skinned; wrap and freeze leftover turkey. Some markets carry turkey fillets, making it possible to buy only as little as you need for one meal.

TURKEY WITH TUNA SAUCE

Turkey, veal, or chicken with tuna sauce is a summer dish found in all parts of Italy. This memorable sauce can also dress hard-cooked eggs or prawns.

1/2 small turkey breast, boned and
    skinned, or 2 fillets
2 tablespoons olive oil
1 inner celery stalk
1 unpeeled carrot
1/2 cup dry white wine
Tuna Sauce (following)

1. Cut turkey breast into 4 long strips. Place strips on a wooden board and slap lightly with the flat side of a chef's knife to flatten.
2. Heat oil in a sauté pan over medium heat, add turkey, and cook until golden brown, about 2 minutes on each side.
3. With a chef's knife, chop celery and carrot coarsely and stir into pan. Pour wine into bottom of pan.
4. Cover and cook over low heat for 10 minutes until tender.
5. Remove turkey to a plate to cool; reserve broth (do not strain) for Tuna Sauce.

TUNA SAUCE

One 7-ounce can solid light tuna,
    packed in olive oil (preferably Italian
    imported tuna), drained
6 anchovy fillets
Reserved broth from pan
4 parsley sprigs (no stems)
2 lemons
1/2 cup mayonnaise (Blender
    Mayonnaise, page 124)
2 tablespoons capers, drained

1. Place drained tuna, anchovies, reserved broth, and parsley in a blender; squeeze in juice of 1 lemon. Purée until smooth and turn out into a bowl.
2. Stir mayonnaise into tuna mixture.
3. Arrange turkey on a plate. Pour sauce over turkey; sprinkle capers over sauce and garnish with lemon. Serve at room temperature.
Serves 2.

TURKEY WITH POMEGRANATE SAUCE

In the Veneto, a region of farmlands and vineyards beyond Venice, when the autumn foliage turns, walnuts, mushrooms, and soft white cheeses come down from the mountains to the markets. I saw ripe pomegranates bursting with juice, tiny new potatoes, chestnuts, small quail, and turkeys from Vicenza.

1/2 small turkey breast, boned and
  skinned, or 2 fillets
2 tablespoons olive oil
1 cup pomegranate juice,* or 1/2 cup
  red currant jelly
2 teaspoons Dijon mustard
1/4 cup honey

1. Cut turkey breast into 4 long strips. Place strips on a wooden board and slap lightly with the flat side of a chef's knife to flatten.
2. Heat oil in a sauté pan over medium heat, add turkey slices, and cook until golden brown, about 2 minutes on each side.
3. Place pomegranate juice in a small saucepan and add mustard and honey. Bring to boil over medium heat, and simmer for 3–4 minutes. As mixture simmers it will become a syrup.
4. When turkey is golden on both sides, pour syrup over turkey in pan. Cover and cook over low heat for 8–10 minutes until tender.
5. Serve turkey hot with sauce from pan.
Serves 2.

*If using a fresh pomegranate, use juicer to extract juice, and strain.

MEAT has always been scarce in Italy, so the Italians know how to make the most of thrifty cuts. Each small piece of veal, beef, lamb, or pork is carefully trimmed of fat and often cooked quickly in a sauté pan or skillet. A tiny scallop of veal is carefully flattened and sautéed with herbs, vegetables, wine, broth, or cream; combined with tuna and mayonnaise; or layered with ham and cheese. A piece of pork is cooked in milk with onions and herbs, or sauced with Marsala.

Boiled meats are very popular in Italy; tongue, beef, and pork sausage are cut in thick slices and served with spicy sauces. Tuscany and Piedmont have good beef; the flavor of a tender steak is heightened by simple cooking: it is quickly seared over high heat, served garnished with lemon and coarsely ground pepper, and accompanied with good Chianti wine and a salad. Italians like young tender lamb at Easter; the sweet meat needs little seasoning except a sprig of rosemary; mature lamb is prepared with garlic and herbs, cheese, and bread crumbs.

Remember:
- Cook thin steaks and patties of beef over high heat, and turn them quickly.
- Always turn meat with a spatula rather than a fork, or you will pierce the meat and lose precious juices.
- Turn meat only once while cooking.
- Do not salt meat before cooking; season with salt once it is turned.
- Veal scallops should not be too thick. Cut thin scallops from fillet or top of leg. Before cooking, slap lightly with the flat side of a chef's knife to thin and flatten each piece of veal. Make shallow slashes on the edges of the scallops so they will lie flat while cooking.
- Veal and pork should never be served rare.

VEAL CHOPS WITH BRANDY

Venice always maintains a romantic illusion for me; the color of the sea, change of weather and season add to the mood. Sitting outside in Piazza San Marco with the orchestra playing casts a spell; even late at night, after the people and pigeons have left, it is romantic.

Two 1/2-inch-thick veal rib chops
1 tablespoon unsalted butter
2 tablespoons brandy
1/2 cup heavy cream
Freshly ground black pepper

1. With a sharp knife, trim fat from veal chops.
2. Heat butter to foaming in a sauté pan, add veal, and cook until brown, about 2 minutes on each side.
3. Stir brandy into pan and ignite. When flame dies, pour cream into pan; season to taste with pepper. Bring to boil over high heat and cook, stirring as sauce thickens, about 3 minutes.
4. Serve veal chops hot on a warm plate with sauce from pan.
Serves 2.

VEAL SCALLOPS WITH OLIVES

Rome at night is flooded with light; all of the ancient, glorious buildings are illuminated; amber-colored monuments, statues, and flowing fountains turn into shadows of history and art. The imposing Piazza del Popolo has twin churches and twin lion fountains. An old and established restaurant nearby serves some of the best dishes in Rome, and the crowd is interesting to watch.

6 thin veal scallops (preferably cut from fillet*)
1 tablespoon olive oil
1/4 cup chopped black olives
3 tablespoons dry white wine
Sea salt
Freshly ground black pepper
10 whole black olives

1. With a sharp knife, trim fat from veal scallops; slash edges with small cuts. Place scallops on a wooden board and slap lightly with the flat side of a chef's knife to flatten.
2. Heat oil in a sauté pan over medium heat, add scallops, and cook until golden, about 1 minute on each side.
3. Lower heat, stir chopped olives into pan, and cook with veal for 1 minute.
4. Stir wine into bottom of pan and season to taste. Add whole olives and cook for 3 minutes.
5. Serve veal hot on a warm plate with olives and sauce from pan.
Serves 2.

*A veal fillet makes small, tender scallops. The scallops will have less fat, need less pounding, and cost less in the long run. Buy a whole fillet, keep it in the freezer, and slice thin scallops as they are needed.

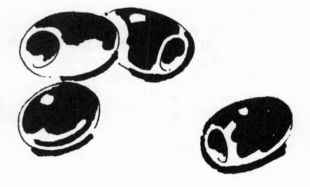

VEAL SCALLOPS WITH FONTINA

6 thin veal scallops (preferably cut from
   fillet)
2 tablespoons unsalted butter
1/4 teaspoon dried oregano
3 thin slices fontina cheese
1/4 cup dry white wine
Freshly ground black pepper
1 lemon

1. With a sharp knife, trim fat from veal
scallops; slash edges with small cuts.
Place scallops on a wooden board and
slap lightly with the flat side of a chef's
knife to flatten.
2. Melt butter in a sauté pan over
medium heat, add oregano, and stir a
few seconds to flavor butter.
3. Add scallops and cook until golden,
about 1 minute on each side.
4. Cut cheese slices to match veal
scallops; place a piece of cheese on
top of each scallop. Pour wine into
bottom of pan, stirring.
5. Lower heat and cook slowly for 3
minutes; season to taste with pepper.
6. Serve veal hot on a warm plate with
sauce from pan; garnish with lemon.
Serves 2.

VENETIAN LIVER

Harry's Bar in Venice is always animated
and crowded; I adore the snacks of
melted cheese, the drinks of champagne
with fresh peach or grape juice, and the
perfectly prepared food.

1 tablespoon unsalted butter
2 tablespoons olive oil
2 yellow onions
1/2 pound best-quality calf's or veal
   liver, very thinly sliced*
1 teaspoon dried sage
Sea salt
Freshly ground black pepper

1. Heat butter and oil in a sauté pan
over medium heat. Slice onions very
thin and stir into pan; cook, stirring, for
2 minutes.
2. Cover pan and cook over low heat
for 5 minutes.
3. Add liver to pan and cook very
briefly, turning once (should be pink
inside).
4. Stir sage into pan and season to
taste. Serve liver hot on a warm plate
with onions.
Serves 2.

*Liver must be sliced very thin.

POACHED BEEF WITH TWO SAUCES

In Italy poached beef is stylishly presented with sauces of Italian colors: a
green herb sauce, a white horseradish
sauce, and a red tomato sauce. Whole
fruits are served in an amber mustard
sauce, sweetened with fruit syrup.

4 cups beef broth
2 unpeeled small carrots
2 unpeeled small turnips, or 2 celery
  stalks
1/2 pound beef fillet
Watercress
Green Sauce and Red Sauce (following)

1. Bring broth to boil in a saucepan
large enough to hold the beef.
2. Put carrots and turnips in broth and
boil for 5 minutes.
3. Lower heat to simmer. Place meat in
broth and cook about 8 minutes; the
meat must be rare for this dish.
4. Remove meat and vegetables to a
warm plate. (Refrigerate broth for another
use.) Garnish with watercress. Serve
hot with Green Sauce and Red Sauce
at table.
Serves 2.

GREEN SAUCE

10 parsley sprigs (no stems)
1/2 shallot, peeled
1 garlic clove, peeled (optional)
2 tablespoons red wine vinegar
1/4 cup olive oil
1 lemon
2 tablespons capers, drained
Freshly ground black pepper

1. Place parsley, shallot, garlic, and
vinegar in a blender and briefly purée.
2. With motor running, slowly add oil in
a thin stream.
3. Pour sauce into a bowl; squeeze in
juice of lemon and stir in capers.
Season to taste with pepper. Serve at
room temperature.
Makes about 3/4 cup.

Very good over gently cooked vegetables
such as broccoli, asparagus, and green
beans.

RED SAUCE

3 unpeeled ripe tomatoes
1/2 sweet red or green pepper
6 parsley sprigs (no stems)
1 cup mayonnaise (Blender Mayonnaise, page 124)

1. Slice tomatoes into a sauté pan and place over medium heat; cover and cook for 5 minutes.
2. Remove lid; cook over high heat, stirring, until the purée is thick. Remove from heat and cool.
3. With a chef's knife, coarsely chop pepper and parsley; mix with mayonnaise in a bowl.
4. Stir cooled tomato purée into mayonnaise and blend well. Serve at room temperature.
Makes about 1-1/2 cups.

SIRLOIN OF BEEF WITH MUSHROOMS

1 egg
1/2 pound ground sirloin
1/4 cup grated Parmesan cheese
1 tablespoon flour
1 tablespoon olive oil
4 unpeeled fresh mushrooms
2 tablespoons Marsala wine
1/4 cup chicken or beef broth
Freshly ground black pepper

1. Break egg into a bowl; mix with a fork or whisk.
2. Add meat and cheese to bowl and combine with egg; form into 2 thick patties and dust with flour on both sides.
3. Heat oil in a sauté pan over medium heat, add meat, and cook about 2 minutes on each side until brown and crusty.
4. Slice mushrooms into pan; stirring, add Marsala and cook for 1 minute.
5. Pour broth into bottom of pan and bring to boil over high heat; lower heat and simmer for 3 minutes. Season to taste with pepper.
6. Serve meat hot on a warm plate with mushrooms and sauce from pan.
Serves 2.

FILLET OF BEEF WITH VERMOUTH

A lovely villa overlooking Florence has gardens laid out in the seventeenth century; the green paths were designed for strolling; there is a *teatro verdura,* a theatre cut from clipped yews and ilex.

2 small 1-inch-thick beef fillets
1 tablespoon unsalted butter
1/4 cup green olives, pitted
1/4 cup sweet red vermouth
Freshly ground black pepper

1. With a sharp knife, trim all fat from fillets.
2. Melt butter in a sauté pan over medium heat, add fillets, and cook until brown, about 2 minutes on each side.
3. Chop olives and stir into pan. Add vermouth and season to taste with pepper. Cook over medium heat for 2–3 minutes until fillets are the desired rareness.
4. Serve fillets hot on a warm plate with sauce from pan.
Serves 2.

ROMAN LAMB CHOPS

Two 1/2-inch-thick lamb chops
1 slice soft white bread
1 egg
2 thin slices fontina or Gruyère cheese
1 tablespoon olive oil
Freshly ground black pepper
1 lemon

1. With a sharp knife, remove fat and bone from lamb chops. Place lamb on a wooden board and slap lightly with the flat side of a chef's knife to flatten.
2. Put bread in a blender to make fine crumbs; spread crumbs on a piece of waxed paper. Break egg into a small bowl and mix with a fork or whisk.
3. Lay a slice of cheese on top of each piece of lamb, dip in beaten egg, then cover well with bread crumbs on both sides.
4. Heat oil in a sauté pan over medium heat; carefully place lamb in oil. Cook lamb until golden brown, about 2 minutes on each side. Season to taste with pepper.
5. Serve lamb hot on a warm plate; garnish with lemon.
Serves 2.

Good with fresh garden peas.

LAMB CHOPS WITH GARLIC

1 tablespoon olive oil
2 loin lamb chops
8 unpeeled garlic cloves
1/4 teaspoon dried thyme
1/4 cup chicken broth
Freshly ground black pepper

1. Heat oil in a sauté pan over medium heat, add lamb, and cook until brown, about 3 minutes on each side.
2. Add garlic cloves and thyme, lower heat, and cook lamb about 3 minutes on each side for rare.
3. Raise heat, add broth, and boil for 1 minute; season to taste with pepper.
4. Serve lamb hot on a warm plate with garlic cloves while sauce is still bubbling. Serves 2.

LAMB ON SKEWERS WITH HERBS

1/2 pound lean lamb from leg
4 slices pancetta (Italian bacon) or lean bacon
Fresh mint leaves, or 1 teaspoon dried rosemary
1 tablespoon olive oil
Freshly ground black pepper

Preheat broiler at full broil
1. Cut lamb into six 2-inch cubes. Cut pancetta into strips to match lamb cubes.
2. On thin wooden skewers, alternate lamb, pancetta, and mint leaves. (If using rosemary, sprinkle over lamb.) Place skewers on an oven sheet and brush with oil.
3. Put lamb under *preheated* broiler and cook for 10 minutes, turning as lamb browns.
4. Season to taste with pepper. Serve lamb hot on a warm plate. Serves 2.

PORK CHOPS MARSALA

There are subtle varieties of Marsala: some are dry and classic in taste; others rich and sweet make perfect dessert wines. Marsala has been known since the time of Caesar as a wine for sipping and for fine cooking. It is one of the world's best-known fortified wines.

Two 1/2-inch-thick center-cut pork
   chops
2 teaspoons unsalted butter
1 teaspoon dried rosemary
1 unpeeled ripe tomato
1/2 cup Marsala wine
Freshly ground black pepper

1. With a sharp knife, trim all fat from pork chops.
2. Melt butter in a sauté pan over medium heat, add rosemary, and stir a few seconds to flavor butter.
3. Place pork chops in pan and cook about 3 minutes on each side, turning as they brown.
4. Slice tomato into pan; stirring, add Marsala and bring to boil. Season to taste with pepper. Cover pan, lower heat, and simmer for 5 minutes.
5. Serve pork hot on a warm plate with sauce from pan.
Serves 2.

BROILED PORK CHOPS WITH LEMON

Two 1/2-inch-thick center-cut pork
  chops
1 tablespoon olive oil
1 lemon
1/4 teaspoon dried oregano
Freshly ground black pepper

Preheat broiler at full broil
1. With a sharp knife, trim all fat from
pork chops; rub with oil on both sides.
2. Place chops on an oven sheet;
squeeze juice of 1/2 lemon over chops
and sprinkle with oregano.
3. Place chops under *preheated* broiler
to cook about 5 minutes.
4. When golden brown, turn chops and
squeeze 1/2 lemon over; cook about 3
minutes until tender.
5. Season to taste with pepper and
serve hot on a warm plate.
Serves 2.

PORK COOKED IN MILK

The Italians cook pork and veal in milk;
they believe it makes the meat tender. I
find the milk makes a velvety sauce,
and the meat tastes like butter.

Two 1/2-inch-thick center-cut pork
  chops (or cut from fillet)
1 tablespoon unsalted butter
1 small yellow onion
1/2 teaspoon dried thyme
1 cup milk
Freshly ground black pepper

1. With a sharp knife, remove fat and
bone from pork chops.
2. Melt butter in a sauté pan over
medium heat, add pork, and cook until
brown, about 3 minutes on each side.
3. Slice onion very thin and stir into
pan; cook in butter for 2 minutes.
Sprinkle thyme over pork and onion.
4. Pour milk into pan and season to
taste with pepper. Turn heat to high
and allow milk to boil for a few seconds.
Lower heat to simmer, cover pan, and
cook for 10 minutes until pork is tender
and onions are very soft; the milk will
have thickened.
5. Serve pork hot on a warm plate with
sauce from pan.
Serves 2.

HAM WITH HONEY AND APPLES

The ancient Romans emphasized choosing the right bouquet of herbs: oregano, fennel, fig leaves for cooking meat. A recipe from an old book calls for fresh ham baked in a crust of flour and oil, and flavored with dried figs, honey, and bay leaves. Ham has always been highly prized in Italy, both cured and fresh.

Two 1-inch-thick ham slices
1 teaspoon unsalted butter
1 unpeeled green apple
2 tablespoons honey
1/2 cup apple juice, or juice of 1
   orange

1. With a sharp knife, trim all fat from ham slices.
2. Melt butter in a sauté pan over medium heat, add ham, and cook until brown, about 2 minutes on each side.
3. Slice apple very thin into pan. Combine honey and apple juice and pour over ham and apple slices.
4. Cover pan and cook over medium heat for 10 minutes.
5. Serve ham hot on a warm plate with apples and sauce from pan.
Serves 2.

KIDNEYS WITH WALNUTS

The Florentines are proud of their fine meat and game; Tuscan cooks use the best raw materials with a minimum of sauces and seasonings. Delicious local food can be sampled in a trattoria or *buca* (cellar).

3 lamb or veal kidneys
1 tablespoon unsalted butter
2 bay leaves
1 tablespoon chopped walnuts
2 tablespoons whiskey or brandy

1. With a sharp knife, slice each kidney into 3–4 slices; remove any membrane or fat.
2. Melt butter in a sauté pan over medium heat. Crumble bay leaves into pan and stir a few seconds to flavor butter.
3. Add kidney slices to pan and cook for 1 minute.
4. Stir chopped walnuts and whiskey into pan. Turn kidney slices to cook evenly. The total cooking time must be no more than 3 minutes, or the kidneys will toughen.
5. Serve kidneys hot on a warm plate with sauce from pan.
Serves 2.

ITALIAN SAUSAGE CAPRI

In the meat markets I saw garlands of spicy sausages hanging with large bunches of dried herbs, prosciutto hams, salamis, and wreaths of red peppers.

These sausages can be found in most Italian markets; they are pure pork and made with various seasonings: some hot with spices, others mildly flavored with fennel. Any sausage, French, Spanish, or English, can be successfully cooked with this recipe.

4 Italian sausages
1/4 cup red wine vinegar
1 teaspoon dried thyme
1 unpeeled ripe tomato

1. Arrange sausages in a sauté pan and place over medium heat. Cook for 5 minutes, turning with a fork to brown evenly. Pour out any fat.
2. Add vinegar and thyme to pan. Slice tomato into pan.
3. Lower heat and cook for 8 minutes, mashing tomato with a spoon as it cooks.
4. Serve sausages hot on a warm plate with sauce from pan.
Serves 2.

VEGETABLES can be prepared in many delightful ways and should be a major part of the diet, as they are in Italy where they are usually treated as a separate course. In Italy you find tender peas cooked with ham, stuffed purple eggplants, carrots flavored with Marsala wine, and small vegetables cut into slices and quickly sautéed in olive oil. Whole stuffed vegetables and vegetable puddings are baked in the oven and sometimes served with a sauce; these dishes can take the place of meat, fowl, or fish at a meal.

Italians are very particular about the size, taste, and texture of their vegetables. The open market in Rome by the Palazzo Farnese has stalls covered with large white umbrellas to shelter the fruit and hundreds of beautiful vegetables that arrive fresh everyday. In late summer there are wooden crates tightly packed with bright yellow zucchini flowers, small finger-size zucchini, large golden cauliflowers, red-and-white bean pods, tiny lavender turnips, and stalks of brussels sprouts. In October, marble-sized pale grapes with stems and leaves are displayed next to red pears, pumpkins, and long yellow-orange squash.

Remember:
- Do not cover pan when cooking green vegetables, as they will turn yellow.
- Do not overcook vegetables; use as little water as possible to retain color and flavor.
- Do not add baking soda to cooking water, as it will reduce vitamin content.
- Do not soak vegetables in water when washing; they will absorb water and lose their taste.

SOME VEGETABLE TIPS

● Keep chopped frozen spinach on the freezer shelf to make instant soups and to combine with meat, eggs, and ricotta cheese.

● Buy artichokes that are firm and green without brown spots.

● Buy small zucchini; large ones can be bitter. If unavailable, substitute yellow squash.

● Frozen peas are a better substitute for fresh than canned.

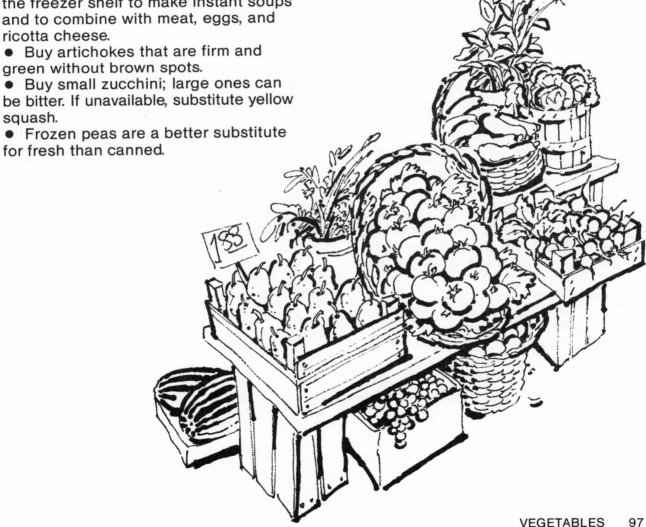

WHITE BEANS WITH SPINACH

A country restaurant near Orvieto offers home-grown vegetables; in the fall there are truffles and small birds served with polenta. The food on the countrified menu is some of the best.

1 bunch fresh spinach, or 1/2 package (about 5 ounces) frozen spinach
1 tablespoon olive oil
1 teaspoon dried sage
1 cup canned cannellini beans (white kidney beans), drained
Freshly ground black pepper

1. With a chef's knife, cut off spinach stems before untying bunch. Wash leaves under cold running water and place in a sauté pan with only the water clinging to the leaves.
2. Bring spinach to boil over high heat, stir, and cook for 2 minutes until leaves wilt.
3. Add oil to pan; stir sage and beans into spinach and cook over medium heat for 2–3 minutes until well mixed.
4. Season to taste with pepper. Serve at room temperature.
Serves 2.

CARROTS MARSALA

1 tablespoon unsalted butter
4 unpeeled small carrots
1/4 cup Marsala wine
2 parsley sprigs (no stems)

1. Melt butter in a sauté pan over medium heat. Slice carrots thinly into pan, stir, and cook slowly for 2 minutes.
2. Pour Marsala into pan; cover pan and cook gently until carrots are tender and liquid is reduced, about 3–4 minutes. If needed, add a tablespoon of water or chicken broth.
3. Chop parsley and sprinkle over carrots. Serve at room temperature.
Serves 2.

GRATED CARROTS

Easy, fast, and colorful.

3 unpeeled small carrots
3 tablespoons chicken broth
3 parsley sprigs (no stems)

1. Grate carrots into a sauté pan; place pan over medium heat.
2. Stir broth into pan and simmer carrots for 2–3 minutes until tender.
3. Chop parsley coarsely and mix into carrots. Serve at room temperature.
Serves 2.

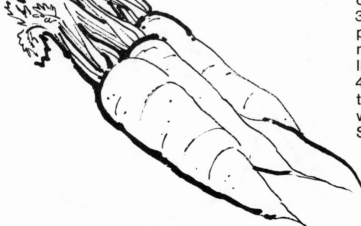

PEAS WITH PROSCIUTTO

Winter is over quickly in Sicily. The tender Sicilian peas arrive early in the markets; they are the sign of spring.

3/4 cup chicken broth
2 lettuce leaves
1 cup fresh shelled peas, or
   1/2 package (about 5 ounces)
   frozen peas
2–3 thin slices prosciutto or boiled ham
Freshly ground black pepper

1. Place broth in a sauté pan and bring to boil over high heat.
2. With a chef's knife, slice lettuce leaves. Stir into boiling broth; add peas and cook rapidly for 2–3 minutes. When peas are barely tender, place contents of pan in a serving bowl.
3. Cut prosciutto into thin strips and place in same sauté pan. Sauté over medium heat for 1–2 minutes until lightly golden.
4. Add prosciutto to peas and season to taste with pepper. Toss gently to mix well. Serve hot or at room temperature.
Serves 2.

BAKED TOMATOES

Add color to most meat and chicken dishes.

2 unpeeled firm ripe tomatoes
2 tablespoons olive oil
1 slice fresh white bread
1 teaspoon dried basil or oregano

Preheat oven to 400°F
1. Cut tomatoes in half crosswise and place in an oven dish. Drizzle oil over tomatoes.
2. Put bread and basil in a blender to make fine crumbs. Sprinkle crumbs over tomato halves.
3. Place tomatoes in *preheated* oven for 10 minutes. Serve at room temperature.
Serves 2.

BAKED HEADS OF GARLIC

2 unpeeled whole heads of garlic (or any number you like)

Preheat oven to 400°F
1. Place garlic heads on an oven sheet and put into *preheated* oven.
2. Bake for 15–20 minutes until garlic cloves are soft. Remove from the oven and cool slightly before peeling. Serve hot with lamb or pork.
Serves 2.

GRATED SQUASH SAUTE

We drove to a house in the Roman countryside for a summer weekend. The garden was full of brilliant color, with dahlias, asters, chrysanthemums, and zinnias in every shade to take the eye; roses filled the air with scent, and you could hear the hum of bees in the hot midday. There was a small fountain, the sound of running water cooling and pleasing to hear; we ate our lunch in a nearby arbor covered with jasmine.

2 unpeeled small zucchini
2 unpeeled green summer squash
2 unpeeled yellow squash
1/4 cup chicken broth
Freshly ground black pepper

1. Grate all of the squash into a sauté pan. Cook over medium heat, stirring, for 2 minutes.
2. Add broth and simmer over low heat for 3 minutes until vegetables are soft.
3. Season to taste with pepper; serve at room temperature.
Serves 2.

Note: You can use any squash in season, alone or a mixture of two or three.

CELERY PUREE

The Tiber Valley is rich in vegetables: celery, tomatoes, onions, mushrooms.

One 14-ounce can celery hearts
6 parsley sprigs (no stems)
1/2 yellow onion, or 1 shallot, peeled
1/2 cup instant mashed potato mix
Freshly ground black pepper

1. Place celery hearts with juice, parsley, and onion in a blender and purée until smooth, about 1 minute.
2. Pour celery mixture into a saucepan, place over medium heat, and cook for 2 minutes. Add potato mix, 1 tablespoon at a time, and cook, stirring, for 2–3 minutes.
3. Season to taste with pepper and serve hot.
Serves 2.

ASPARAGUS PARMESAN

2 cups water
12 asparagus spears*
1 tablespoon olive oil
1/4 cup grated Parmesan cheese
Freshly ground black pepper

Preheat oven to 375°F
1. Place water in a sauté pan and bring to boil over high heat.
2. Cut off and discard tough ends of asparagus and peel stalks. Place in boiling water and cook rapidly for 3–4 minutes until barely tender.
3. Drain asparagus and arrange in an oven dish. Pour oil over tips and sprinkle with cheese.
4. Place in *preheated* oven about 1–2 minutes until cheese is golden brown.
5. Season to taste with pepper and serve hot.
Serves 2.

*When cleaning asparagus, cut off tough part of stems and remove scales with a sharp knife; dirt catches under the scales.

GREEN BEANS WITH CHEESE

For me, a temporary Florentine, it was a wonderful winter. From my apartment I had a view of the soaring red dome of the cathedral and the Baptistry doors. Florence was alive with activity: statues and paintings that had been removed and hidden during World War II were being reinstalled throughout the city; there were masterpieces everywhere.

1 cup chicken broth
2 lettuce leaves
1/2 pound fresh green beans, or
   1/2 package (about 5 ounces) frozen green beans
1/4 cup grated Parmesan cheese
Freshly ground black pepper

1. Place broth in a sauté pan and bring to boil over high heat.
2. With a chef's knife, slice lettuce leaves and add to broth.
3. Snap ends from green beans and remove any strings; chop coarsely. Add beans to boiling broth; cook rapidly for 2–3 minutes until barely tender.
4. Place contents of pan in a serving bowl. Sprinkle with cheese and season to taste with pepper. Toss gently to mix well. Serve at room temperature.
Serves 2.

BROCCOLI AND ZUCCHINI

The trick is to pour the oil and lemon over the vegetables when freshly cooked, drained, and warm.

2 cups chicken broth
2 stalks broccoli
3 unpeeled small zucchini
1 lemon
2 tablespoons olive oil (optional)
Freshly ground black pepper
4 parsley sprigs (no stems)

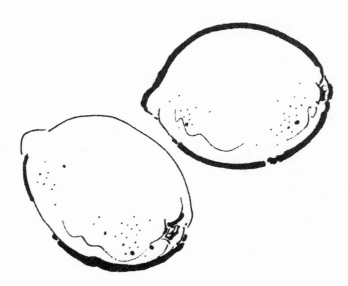

1. Place broth in a sauté pan and bring to boil over high heat.
2. With a chef's knife, remove tough ends of broccoli and discard; chop broccoli and zucchini coarsely.
3. Lower heat; stir vegetables into simmering broth and cook for 2–3 minutes until tender.
4. Drain broccoli and zucchini and place on a flat plate. (Refrigerate broth for another time.)
5. Squeeze juice of lemon over vegetables, add oil, and season to taste with pepper. Chop parsley and sprinkle over vegetables. Serve at room temperature. Serves 2.

Note: The broth reserved from cooking the vegetables can be used to make soup the next evening. Just add a handful of pastina (tiny soup pasta) or rice.

ARTICHOKES, ROMAN STYLE

A Roman restaurant on the left bank of the Tiber serves artichokes deep-fried in olive oil; they look like large flowers with their petals open. Artichokes cooked in broth with herbs are served with long stems pointing upwards.

On hot summer nights the tiny Piazza Margana is alive with singing and people, very much like an Italian opera.

4 cups chicken broth
2 artichokes
1 lemon
1 teaspoon olive oil
1/2 teaspoon dried oregano
1/2 teaspoon dried thyme

1. Place broth in a saucepan and bring to boil over high heat.
2. With a sharp knife, cut off top half of artichokes and cut artichokes in half lengthwise, leaving stems intact; trim tough leaves. Squeeze juice of lemon over artichokes.
3. Add oil and herbs to boiling broth, lower heat to simmer, and add artichokes.
4. Cook artichokes about 12–15 minutes until tender.
5. Serve at room temperature, sauced with broth.
Serves 2.

LIMA BEANS WITH PROSCIUTTO

1 tablespoon unsalted butter
1/2 teaspoon dried sage
2 thin slices prosciutto
1 cup canned lima beans, or
   1/2 package (about 5 ounces) frozen
   lima beans
1/2 cup chicken broth
Freshly ground black pepper

1. Melt butter in a sauté pan over medium heat, add sage, and stir a few seconds to flavor butter.
2. Cut prosciutto into thin strips, add to pan, and sauté for 1 minute.
3. Stir lima beans into pan, add broth, and simmer for 4–5 minutes until beans are hot and tender.
4. Season to taste with pepper and serve at room temperature.
Serves 2.

Variation: Shelled peas, fresh or frozen, can be used in place of the lima beans.

MUSHROOMS WITH PINE NUTS

1 tablespoon olive oil
6 unpeeled large fresh mushrooms
1/4 cup dry white wine
Freshly ground black pepper
1/4 cup pine nuts

1. Heat oil in a sauté pan over medium heat. Slice mushrooms very thin into pan and cook for 1 minute, stirring in oil.
2. Pour wine into pan; season to taste with pepper and cook over high heat for 2 minutes.
3. Lower heat; stir pine nuts into mushrooms and cook for 1 minute. Serve hot.
Serves 2.

CAULIFLOWER IN WHITE WINE

1 small cauliflower
1/4 cup olive oil
1 cup dry white wine
Sea salt
Freshly ground black pepper
4 parsley sprigs (no stems)

1. With a chef's knife, chop cauliflower coarsely.
2. Heat oil in a sauté pan over medium heat, stir cauliflower into oil, and cook for 2–3 minutes.
3. Pour wine into pan and season to taste. Cover pan and simmer for 10 minutes.
4. Chop parsley and sprinkle over cauliflower. Serve cauliflower at room temperature with broth from pan.
Serves 2.

BRUSSELS SPROUTS WITH CHESTNUTS

Natural peeled chestnuts can be found in a jar or can on the market shelf.

2 cups beef broth
1 celery stalk
1/2 cup brussels sprouts
1 lemon
1/2 cup peeled chestnuts, drained
Freshly ground black pepper

1. Place broth in a sauté pan and bring to boil over high heat.
2. Lower heat; stir celery stalk and brussels sprouts into simmering broth. Cut 3 strips lemon rind into pan and cook for 5 minutes.
3. Add chestnuts and simmer for 5–6 minutes until brussels sprouts are tender. Discard celery stalk.
4. Season to taste with pepper. Toss gently to mix well and serve hot.
Serves 2.

BAKED POTATOES

4 unpeeled small red rose potatoes
1 cup heavy cream
1/2 cup grated Parmesan cheese
Ground nutmeg

Preheat oven to 400°F
1. Slice washed potatoes very thin and place in a 6 X 9-inch oven dish.
2. Pour cream over potatoes and sprinkle with cheese. Dust with nutmeg to taste.
3. Bake potatoes in *preheated* oven for 15 minutes, or until tender. Serve hot.
Serves 2.

POTATOES WITH BROTH

4 unpeeled small red rose potatoes
2 tablespoons olive oil
1 garlic clove, peeled
1 teaspoon dried rosemary
1/2 cup chicken broth
Freshly ground black pepper

1. With a chef's knife, chop washed potatoes coarsely.
2. Heat oil in a sauté pan over medium heat, add garlic and rosemary, and stir a few seconds to flavor oil.
3. Add potatoes to pan and cook over medium heat, stirring, for 2–3 minutes.
4. Stir broth into pan and season to taste with pepper. Discard garlic clove.
5. Cook potatoes over low heat until tender, about 10 minutes, stirring as they cook. The potatoes should be moist when done. Serve hot.
Serves 2.

POTATO PUDDING

The high points of my eating experience have involved the most basic foods perfectly prepared and presented: a golden chicken, a soft green salad, a crisp potato pancake.

Try this simple dish.

1 cup water
1/3 cup milk
1 cup instant mashed potato mix
1/2 cup grated fontina, bel paese, or
 Swiss cheese
Freshly ground black pepper

Preheat oven to 425°F
1. Pour water into a saucepan and bring to boil over high heat. Add milk and pour into a bowl.
2. Stir potato mix into bowl and quickly mix until creamy.
3. Generously butter a 6 X 9-inch oven dish. Sprinkle 1/4 cup grated cheese on the bottom; spread potato mixture evenly over cheese, smoothing the top with a spatula. Sprinkle 1/4 cup grated cheese on top and season to taste with pepper.
4. Bake in *preheated* oven for 10–12 minutes until golden brown. Serve hot. Serves 2.

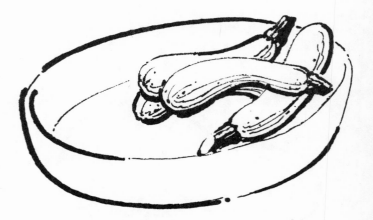

ZUCCHINI PUDDING

A vegetable pudding can be the star of a meal.

1/2 cup grated fontina or Gruyère
    cheese
4 unpeeled small zucchini
2 eggs, at room temperature
1 cup crème fraîche (homemade,
    page 23) or 1/2 cup *each* milk and
    heavy cream
Freshly ground black pepper
Tomato Sauce (following)

Preheat oven to 350°F
1. Generously butter a 6 X 9-inch oven dish. Sprinkle 1/4 cup grated cheese on the bottom; slice zucchini and spread evenly over cheese.
2. Break eggs into a bowl and beat until frothy with a whisk or egg beater. Stir crème fraîche and 1/4 cup grated cheese into bowl and season to taste with pepper.
3. Pour egg mixture over zucchini in oven dish; bake in *preheated* oven for 15 minutes until custard is set. Do not overcook.
4. Serve at room temperature with Tomato Sauce.
Serves 2.

TOMATO SAUCE

2 unpeeled ripe tomatoes, or 2 canned
    Italian plum tomatoes
1 orange
1/2 cup Marsala wine

1. Slice tomatoes into a sauté pan and place over medium heat. Cut 4 strips orange rind into pan and squeeze in juice of orange.
2. Stir Marsala into mixture, cover pan, and simmer for 5 minutes.
3. Remove cover and stir sauce, mashing tomatoes to make a thick purée; do not overcook. Serve at room temperature. Makes about 2 cups.

PUMPKIN PUDDING

Good with chicken or pork dishes.

2 eggs, at room temperature
1 teaspoon dried basil*
1 cup milk
Freshly ground black pepper
1 cup canned pumpkin purée
1/4 cup grated Parmesan cheese

Preheat oven to 350°F
1. Break eggs into a bowl and beat with a whisk or egg beater until well mixed. Stir in basil, milk, and pepper to taste.
2. Stir pumpkin purée into eggs, mixing well.
3. Pour pumpkin mixture into a buttered 6 X 9-inch oven dish and sprinkle grated cheese over the top. Bake in *preheated* oven for 10 minutes until just set; do not overcook. Serve hot or at room temperature.
Serves 2.

*Basil and pumpkin are two flavors that complement each other.

BROCCOLI PUDDING

1-1/2 cups water
2 stalks broccoli
1 cup instant mashed potato mix
2 eggs, at room temperature
1/2 cup milk
1/2 cup grated Parmesan, Gruyère, or fontina cheese

Preheat oven to 400°F
1. Place water in a sauté pan and bring to boil over high heat.
2. With a chef's knife, cut off tough ends of broccoli and discard. Chop broccoli coarsely and add to boiling water. Cook for 3 minutes.
3. Put potato mix in a bowl and pour 1 cup boiling water from broccoli into bowl; stir briefly until well mixed.
4. Drain broccoli, put in a blender, and purée until smooth.
5. Break eggs into a bowl and beat until frothy with a whisk or egg beater; stir in milk, cheese, potato mixture, and broccoli purée, mixing well.
6. Turn into a buttered 6 X 9-inch oven dish and bake in *preheated* oven for 10 minutes until puffed and golden.
Serve hot.
Serves 2.

ONIONS, ROMAN STYLE

The ancient Roman sour-sweet sauces (*agrodolce*) are still used in Rome today. In old cookbooks the sauce contains pine nuts, honey, vinegar, oil, and wine. *Agrodolce* sauces are used with duck, zucchini, cabbage, onions, and carrots.

2 tablespoons olive oil
1 cup canned small white onions, drained
1/2 cup Marsala wine
1/4 cup red wine vinegar
1 tablespoon firmly packed brown sugar
1/4 cup raisins or dried currants

1. Heat oil in a saucepan over medium heat and stir onions into oil.
2. Lower heat and simmer onions gently for 3 minutes.
3. In a bowl combine Marsala, vinegar, sugar, and raisins; stir into pan.
4. Cook onions slowly about 7 minutes until sauce becomes like a syrup.
5. Serve at room temperature.
Serves 2.

SALADS can be made with a mixture of tender seasonal greens, good oil, and lemon juice or vinegar. In October, the farmer's market in Rome has baskets of young spinach leaves, bulbs of fennel with feathery green tops, endive, and special red *radicchio*. Formed like romaine lettuce, *radicchio* has dark red leaves with white veins; it makes a delicate salad.

In Italy, salad is not served as a separate course. A green salad is usually combined with sliced tomatoes, shredded celery, and carrots. Cooked vegetables (green beans, spinach, and broccoli) often appear at room temperature as an antipasto. Raw vegetables (endive, fennel, and mushrooms) seasoned with oil and lemon are served at the beginning of the meal. This simple, natural treatment of cooked and raw vegetables makes good sense, as the vegetables retain their vitamins and fresh taste.

Remember:
- Oil and vinegar, like all seasonings, are a matter of taste and preference. For a salad, a fine olive oil is always best.
- Unflavored red or white wine vinegar is mixed with oil for dressings. Often fresh lemon juice is used in place of vinegar as it adds a light taste to vegetables.
- Freshly ground black pepper is the final touch. Flakes of sea salt, or coarsely ground salt, may be added for texture.
- In Italy I am never aware of sharpness in a salad dressing, only a blend of seasonings that enhances the vegetables and greens.

GREEN SALAD

1 small head butter lettuce, romaine
    lettuce, or other salad greens
Dressings (pages 122–24)

1. Wash lettuce leaves quickly under cold running water; drain into a colander.
2. Wrap lettuce leaves in a paper towel and refrigerate in the vegetable compartment until ready to make salad. The leaves must be dry, or the dressing will not cling to them.
3. Just before serving, tear and toss lettuce with dressing, gently turning the leaves over and over so that each is coated with a thin film of dressing. Do not serve the salad chilled, or the flavor will be lost.
Serves 2.

Note: I sometimes use only the tender inner leaves of lettuce for salad. Save the outer leaves; they add flavor when cooking vegetables and soups.

FENNEL WITH OIL AND LEMON

In Italy fennel is brought to the table in a bowl of water; it is served with oil and lemon. Celery can also be used.

1 small bulb fennel with feathery leaves
1 lemon
1/4 cup olive oil
Freshly ground black pepper
Sea salt

1. Slice fennel bulb thin and place in a bowl; squeeze juice of lemon over.
2. With a chef's knife, chop feathery tops very fine and add to bowl.
3. Pour oil into bowl and season to taste. Toss carefully to mix well. Serve at room temperature.
Serves 2.

Variation: Add 1/4 cup grated fontina or Gruyère cheese before adding oil.

ARTICHOKE SALAD

Very fast and easy; all of the ingredients are on your shelf.

4 canned artichoke hearts, bottoms, or quarters
1 lemon
2 tablespoons olive oil
1 tablespoon capers, drained
6 black olives, pitted
Freshly ground black pepper

1. Slice artichokes lengthwise into a bowl.
2. Squeeze juice of lemon into bowl; stirring, add oil and capers.
3. Slice olives into bowl and toss carefully to mix well.
4. Season to taste with pepper. Serve at room temperature.
Serves 2.

MUSHROOM, CELERY, AND FONTINA SALAD

Boxes of mushrooms, *funghi,* arrive in autumn in the markets. I saw a variety of colors and sizes: white, brown, yellow-orange, and baskets of *porcini* as large as an elephant's ear with fringed edges.

1/2 cup heavy cream
1–2 lemons
8 unpeeled small fresh white mushrooms
2 small inner celery stalks
4 thin slices fontina or Gruyère cheese
Freshly ground black pepper

1. Pour cream into a bowl and squeeze in juice of 1 lemon.
2. Slice mushrooms and celery very thin into bowl and toss immediately with dressing.
3. Cut cheese into long, thin strips; stir into bowl.
4. Add more lemon juice, if needed to thin dressing; season to taste with pepper. Serve at room temperature.
Serves 2.

CAULIFLOWER SALAD

I had this beautifully presented salad in the home of a Roman artist, an intriguing studio filled with exotic jewelry, paintings, and sculpture.

3 cups water
1 small cauliflower
12 tender spinach leaves (no stems)
1 cup crème fraîche (homemade, page 23) or plain yogurt
1 garlic clove, peeled (optional)
8 parsley sprigs (no stems)
1 lemon
Paprika
2 tablespoons capers, drained
6 anchovy fillets (optional)

1. Pour water into a saucepan and place over high heat.
2. Put whole cauliflower with its green leaves in pan; when water boils, lower heat, cover pan, and simmer for 10 minutes until cauliflower is barely tender.
3. Arrange 4 spinach leaves on a flat plate and place cauliflower on leaves.
4. Put 8 spinach leaves, crème fraîche, garlic, and parsley in a blender and purée until smooth. Squeeze in juice of lemon and mix well; season to taste with paprika.
5. Pour spinach sauce over cauliflower; garnish with paprika, capers, and anchovies. Serve at room temperature. Serves 2.

CELERY ROOT SALAD WITH PROSCIUTTO

1 small celery root
1 lemon
4 thin slices prosciutto or boiled ham
1 cup mayonnaise (Blender Mayonnaise, page 124*)
4 parsley sprigs (no stems)
Freshly ground black pepper
Romaine lettuce

1. With a sharp knife, remove outside knobby skin of celery root. Grate celery root into a bowl; squeeze juice of lemon over to prevent discoloration.
2. Cut prosciutto into long, thin strips and add to bowl.
3. Stir mayonnaise into bowl; chop parsley and add, mixing well. Season to taste with pepper.
4. Serve on lettuce leaves at room temperature.
Serves 2.

With crusty bread, cheese, and fruit, this makes a complete meal.

*If making the mayonnaise, use lemon juice rather than vinegar.

WHITE BEAN SALAD

Italian white kidney beans are surrounded with lettuce and garnished with lemon slices.

2 lemons
1 teaspoon Dijon mustard
1/4 cup olive oil
1 cup canned cannellini beans, drained
6 parsley sprigs (no stems)
1/2 cup chopped walnuts
1 small head butter lettuce
Freshly ground black pepper

1. In a bowl combine juice of 1 lemon, mustard, and oil.
2. Place drained beans in bowl.
3. Chop parsley and stir into beans; add chopped walnuts and mix gently.
4. Place small leaves of butter lettuce on a plate and place beans in center. Season to taste with pepper and garnish with lemon. Serve at room temperature.
Serves 2.

FRUIT SALAD
WITH YOGURT DRESSING

A summer salad: use any combination of oranges, nectarines, pears, grapes, peaches.

1 cup plain yogurt
2 tablespoons honey
2 oranges
1 lemon
1 tablespoon fresh mint leaves
   (optional)
1 cup seedless grapes

1. In a bowl combine yogurt with honey. Squeeze in juice of 1 orange and juice of lemon. Chop mint coarsely, add to bowl, and stir dressing, mixing well.
2. Peel orange and slice into bowl. Add grapes and toss carefully to mix well. Serve at room temperature.
Serves 2.

SPINACH WITH OIL AND LEMON

The Italians like salads made with cooked vegetables: spinach, broccoli, and zucchini often appear seasoned with oil and lemon, served at room temperature.

1 bunch fresh spinach, or 1/2 package
   (about 5 ounces) frozen spinach
1 lemon
1–2 tablespoons olive oil
Sea salt
Freshly ground black pepper

1. With a chef's knife, cut off spinach stems before untying bunch. Wash leaves under cold running water and place in a sauté pan with only the water clinging to the leaves.
2. Bring spinach to boil over high heat, stir, and cook for 2 minutes until leaves wilt; drain into a colander.
3. When cool, squeeze spinach with your hands to remove excess moisture, and form into 2 small balls. Place spinach balls on a flat plate.
4. Squeeze juice of lemon over spinach, pour oil over, and season to taste. Serve at room temperature.
Serves 2.

SLICED ORANGES
WITH ANCHOVY DRESSING

1/4 cup red wine vinegar
6 anchovy fillets
1/2 cup olive oil
Freshly ground black pepper
2 oranges
Curly endive or butter lettuce

1. Place vinegar and anchovies in a
small pan over medium heat and stir
until anchovies melt into vinegar, about
1 minute.
2. Add oil to pan and season to taste
with pepper. Heat dressing until hot.
3. Peel oranges and slice very thin into
a bowl. Pour hot dressing over.
4. Tear endive leaves into bowl and
toss carefully to mix well. Serve at
once.
Serves 2.

AMERICAN CHICKEN SALAD

In Trastevere an intimate restaurant
with a fireplace for cold winter days has
a pretty walled garden with umbrellas
for summer dining. I saw this salad on
the menu and was intrigued with the
title—an Italian version of chicken salad.

2 cups chicken broth
1 whole chicken breast, halved, boned,
   and skinned
1 unpeeled small cucumber
2 small inner celery stalks
1 unpeeled small carrot
2 lemons
1/4 cup olive oil
Heart of butter lettuce
Freshly ground black pepper
Radicchio (red winter lettuce, optional)

1. Place broth in a saucepan and bring
to boil over high heat. Lower heat, add
chicken, and simmer for 10 minutes, or
until tender.
2. Slice cucumber in half lengthwise
and remove seeds. With a chef's knife,
chop cucumber and celery coarsely
and place in a bowl.
3. Grate carrot into bowl and squeeze
in juice of 1 lemon. Add oil and stir to
combine well.
4. Remove chicken from broth (refrigerate
broth for another time) and cut into
long, thin strips.
5. Place chicken and heart of lettuce in
bowl with vegetables; squeeze in juice
of 1 lemon and season to taste with
pepper; toss carefully to mix well.
6. If using *radicchio,* cut into long, thin
strips and place over salad. Serve at
room temperature.
Serves 2.

Note: This salad can also be made with
cooked chicken you have on hand; use
1 cup shredded cooked chicken.

PRAWN AND RICE SALAD

Entering Elba by sea you can see a fortress and a castle; the town rises in front of you. We were content to sit in this most serene of places; later we were plunging off rocks into cool water.

When time and energy are short, buy cooked prawns to make this summer meal.

3 cups water
1/2 cup Italian Arborio rice
1/2 cup fresh or frozen shelled peas
1 shallot, peeled
1/4 cup olive oil
1 lemon
1/4 pound cooked cleaned prawns

1. Place water in a saucepan and bring to boil over high heat.
2. Slowly add rice to boiling water, lower heat, and simmer about 10 minutes until rice is tender. Add peas last 5 minutes of cooking time.
3. Drain rice and peas into a strainer; place in a bowl.
4. Chop shallot; stir into warm rice with olive oil and juice of lemon. Toss gently to mix well.
5. Stir prawns into rice. Serve at room temperature.
Serves 2.

TONGUE SALAD

6 slices cooked beef tongue or rare
   beef
2 unpeeled ripe tomatoes
1 shallot, peeled
4 parsley sprigs (no stems)
1 tablespoon red wine vinegar
1 teaspoon Dijon mustard
1/4 cup olive oil
Freshly ground black pepper
1 tablespoon capers, drained
Romaine lettuce

1. Cut tongue into long, thin strips and
place in a bowl.
2. Put tomatoes, shallot, and parsley in
a blender and chop coarsely; place in
bowl with tongue.
3. In a small bowl combine vinegar and
mustard, and stir in oil.
4. Pour dressing over tongue and toss
carefully to mix well. Season to taste
with pepper; garnish with capers.
5. Serve on lettuce leaves at room temperature.
Serves 2.

A simple meal with crusty bread and
cheese.

BASIC DRESSING

1/4 cup red wine vinegar
1/4 teaspoon Dijon mustard (optional,
   for a sharper taste)
Sea salt
Freshly ground black pepper
1/2 cup olive oil

1. In a bowl mix vinegar and mustard;
season to taste.
2. Add oil and stir until well combined.
Makes about 3/4 cup.

LEMON DRESSING

2 lemons
1 teaspoon Dijon mustard (optional, for
   a sharper taste)
Sea salt
Freshly ground black pepper
1/4 cup olive oil

1. Squeeze juice of lemons into a bowl
and stir in mustard. Season to taste.
2. Add oil and stir until well combined.
Makes about 1/2 cup.

GORGONZOLA DRESSING

Try this creamy dressing over romaine lettuce, or over thinly sliced oranges and red onions.

1/4 cup red wine vinegar
1/4 cup crumbled gorgonzola cheese
1/4 cup heavy cream
Freshly ground black pepper

1. In a bowl or blender mix vinegar, cheese, and cream.
2. Season to taste with pepper.
Makes about 3/4 cup.

HERB DRESSING

Try this with thinly sliced mushrooms.

2 lemons
3 tablespoons chopped mixed fresh
  herbs, or 1 tablespoon mixed dried
  herbs (parsley, tarragon, oregano, and
  basil, in any combination)
Freshly ground black pepper
1/2 cup olive oil

1. Squeeze juice of lemons into a bowl and add herbs; season to taste with pepper.
2. Add oil and stir until well combined.
Makes about 3/4 cup.

WALNUT OIL DRESSING

This dressing is good over a salad of endive and seedless grapes, or mixed with thinly sliced mushrooms and chopped parsley.

1/4 cup red wine vinegar
Sea salt
Freshly ground black pepper
1/4 cup coarsely chopped walnuts
1/2 cup walnut oil

1. In a bowl place vinegar; season to taste and stir in walnuts.
2. Add oil and stir until well combined.
Makes about 1 cup.

RICOTTA CHEESE DRESSING

A low-calorie dressing that is good over any lettuce.

1/2 cup ricotta or cottage cheese
2 tablespoons heavy cream or water
4 parsley sprigs (no stems)
Any fresh herbs in season (basil, oregano, mint)
1 lemon
Paprika

1. Combine ricotta, cream, parsley, and herbs in a blender; squeeze in juice of lemon and mix until smooth.
2. Season to taste with paprika.
Makes about 3/4 cup.

MAYONNAISE

Italians like mayonnaise; they combine it with chicken, veal, vegetables. An antipasto might consist of sliced radishes, tomatoes, mushrooms, hard-cooked eggs, tuna, or artichoke hearts, garnished with mayonnaise.

There is neither magic nor mystery in making mayonnaise; anyone can easily prepare it in a blender in seconds.

BLENDER MAYONNAISE

1 egg, at room temperature
1/2–3/4 cup safflower oil (or any light oil)
1 lemon, or 2 tablespoons wine vinegar
Freshly ground black pepper

1. Break egg into a blender and mix for a few seconds.
2. With motor running, slowly add oil in a *thin stream*.
3. As mixture thickens, squeeze juice of lemon into blender. Add oil only until mayonnaise is consistency you like. Thin mayonnaise with more lemon juice (or vinegar) if needed. Turn into a bowl and season to taste with pepper.
Makes about 1 cup.

Here are some variations on the theme:

Pistachio Mayonnaise: To mayonnaise in blender, add 6 parsley sprigs (no stems) and a good handful of shelled pistachio nuts; blend well.

Yogurt Mayonnaise: After turning mayonnaise into a bowl, mix in 1/2 cup plain yogurt. The yogurt lightens the mayonnaise.

ORANGE MAYONNAISE

Lovely with fruit salads and with poached fish.

1 egg, at room temperature
1/2–3/4 cup safflower oil (or any
  light oil)
1 orange
2 teaspoons Dijon mustard
Freshly ground black pepper

1. Break egg into a blender and mix for a few seconds.
2. With motor running, slowly add oil in a *thin stream.*
3. As mixture thickens, squeeze juice of orange into blender. Add oil only until mayonnaise is consistency you like.
4. Turn mayonnaise into a bowl. Grate rind of orange into bowl, add mustard, and mix well. Season to taste with pepper.
Makes about 1 cup.

DESSERT can be any one of a variety of sweets, cookies, cakes, ice cream, pudding, or fruit. Italians usually end a meal with fruit in season or a small piece of cheese, or perhaps fresh walnuts in the fall. Peaches, pears, and grapes may be served in a bowl of cool water at the table, or a basket piled high with fruit is set before diners in a restaurant.

Italians like sweets; there are many pastry shops resembling cafes, with tables inside and on the pavement, where they stop during the day for coffee and cakes. Rich desserts, saved for special occasions, are rarely home-made. On Sundays and holidays, Italians can be seen carrying a box tied with string, filled with pastries for a festive meal. These pastry-shop creations are different from those prepared at home. The shops and restaurants have showy cakes with spun sugar, cream, or meringue; homemade desserts are simple and restrained, perhaps a thin sponge cake decorated with walnut halves or a custard.

Each region of Italy has its own dessert specialty: Bologna favors confections of whipped cream; Naples makes pastries with marzipan and pistachio nuts; each Florentine family has a version of *zuccotto*, a molded dessert of sponge cake and fruit drenched in liqueur. Many desserts are based on centuries of tradition: During Easter week the pastry shops are filled with doves of cake and bread symbolizing new life, and wheat breads baked with colored eggs symbolizing fertility. At Christmas, there are special breads, cakes, and cookies made with sugared fruits and nuts.

PEACHES WITH WINE

I had this simple dessert often in Rome. It is served everywhere when the peaches are ripe and sweet; the wine enhances the flavor of the peach.

2 peaches
1 teaspoon granulated sugar
1/2 cup red or white wine

1. Peel peaches and remove stones; slice into a bowl.
2. Mix sugar with wine and pour over peaches. Serve at room temperature. Serves 2.

PEACHES AND FIGS WITH CREAM

Most Italians like to go to the sea in summer; the Argentario peninsula, not far from Rome, is an enchantment of small bays, rock cliffs, and a fishing village where you can eat on a waterfront terrace overlooking the port. Around Porto Ercole, away from the water, are olive groves, rose-covered pergolas, and fields of lavender; in late summer the peach and fig trees are heavy with ripe fruit.

2 ripe peaches
4 ripe figs, or 1/4 cup fig jam
1 cup heavy cream
1/4 cup powdered sugar
1 teaspoon vanilla extract

1. Peel and slice peaches and figs into a bowl.
2. Pour cream into a bowl and whip with a whisk or egg beater until thickened. Add sugar and vanilla and continue to beat until softly peaked.
3. Fold cream gently into fruit, mixing well. Refrigerate until ready to serve. Serves 2.

This heavenly dessert is also good frozen.

PEARS MARSALA

1 cup water
1/4 cup granulated sugar
2 unpeeled small pears
1 lemon
2 tablespoons red currant jelly
1/2 cup Marsala wine

1. Combine water and sugar in a sauce-pan over high heat, stirring to dissolve sugar. Boil rapidly for 5 minutes to form a syrup.
2. Cut pears in half (if large, cut in quarters). Squeeze juice of lemon over pears.
3. Lower heat and place pears in syrup. Cover pan and simmer for 5–6 minutes until tender when pierced with a fork. Turn pears once during cooking.
4. Remove pears to a dish with a slotted spoon. Add jelly and Marsala to pan and boil rapidly over high heat for 3 minutes.
5. Pour syrup over pears and serve at room temperature.
Serves 2.

CHESTNUTS COOKED IN WINE

When winter is in the air, the smell of roasting chestnuts drifts around the cold, chilly corners; in Italy, chestnuts are usually cooked in the shell and served with a glass of wine.

12–14 chestnuts
1 cup dry white wine

Preheat oven to 450°F
1. With a sharp knife, cut a gash on the flat side of each chestnut.
2. Place chestnuts in an oven dish and pour the wine over them.
3. Place dish in *preheated* oven for 15 minutes.
4. Remove dish from oven and peel shells and inner brown skin from chest-nuts while still warm, as shells are easier to remove. Serve at room tem-perature.
Serves 2.

STRAWBERRIES WITH VINEGAR

In season you can find perfumed small wild strawberries from the Alban hills in the markets and restaurants of Rome. They are served with lemon juice, orange juice, or, best of all, red wine vinegar and sugar. The vinegar well mixed with the sugar is the key that opens the door to the perfume and flavor of the berries; the acidity brings out the taste of the berries and increases the sweetness.

1 cup unwashed strawberries
1 cup red or white wine
2 tablespoons red wine vinegar
2 teaspoons granulated sugar

1. Check berries carefully for any bad spots; leave on green tops and stems.
2. To wash the berries, place them in a small bowl and cover with wine; pour off the wine.
3. In a bowl combine the vinegar and sugar, mixing well. Pour over the berries and stir gently.
4. Keep berries in a cool place until serving time; do not refrigerate, as the cold kills the flavor.
Serves 2.

Note: Italians wash strawberries in wine instead of water, as water destroys the aroma and taste and makes the berries watery.

PERSIMMON PUREE
WITH VANILLA ICE CREAM

When late fall and early winter arrive in Rome, there are many desserts made with persimmon. This bright, shiny fruit has an intense orange color and sweetness.

1 unpeeled ripe persimmon*
1 tablespoon brandy
Granulated sugar (optional)
1 pint vanilla ice cream
Chopped walnuts (optional)

1. Remove stone and place persimmon in a blender. Add brandy and purée until smooth.
2. Taste purée and add sugar, if needed.
3. Put a scoop of ice cream in each serving dish. Spoon purée over ice cream and sprinkle with chopped walnuts, if desired. Serve chilled.
Serves 2.

*When not ripe, a persimmon has an astringent taste; when ripe, the flesh is soft and wet, and intensely sweet.

SLICED FROZEN PERSIMMON

Autumn is the best season of the year for eating; you can still find summer fruits—peaches, raspberries, strawberries, and grapes; you can also find autumn pears, persimmons, and crisp apples.

1 ripe persimmon
Crème fraîche (homemade, page 23), or equal parts sour cream and plain yogurt

1. Freeze the persimmon until firm.
2. Slice unpeeled frozen persimmon very thin and place in a bowl. Serve chilled with a bowl of crème fraîche at table.
Serves 2.

COFFEE ICE CREAM WITH CHESTNUTS

In winter beautiful sugared fruits—huge apricots, pineapple slices, prunes—and glazed chestnuts are found in Italian pastry shops.

1 pint coffee ice cream
1/2 cup whole or broken chestnuts in syrup (available in jars or cans)
1 tablespoon Amaretto or Frangelico liqueur

1. Put a scoop of ice cream in each serving dish.
2. Spoon chestnuts and syrup over ice cream; pour 1/2 tablespoon liqueur over each serving. Serve chilled.
Serves 2.

CHOCOLATE SAUCE WITH CHOCOLATE ICE CREAM

This sauce is adapted from the wonderful *tartufo*, chocolate truffle, found in Rome.

4 squares (4 ounces) semisweet chocolate
1/2 cup hot coffee
1 pint chocolate ice cream
2 teaspoons powdered cocoa

1. Break chocolate into small pieces into a bowl; add coffee.
2. Place bowl in a saucepan of simmering water and stir as chocolate melts.
3. Keep sauce warm over hot water until serving time; if sauce is too thick, add a bit more coffee (or some cognac).
4. To serve, put a scoop of ice cream in each serving dish. Spoon hot chocolate sauce over ice cream; sprinkle 1 teaspoon cocoa over each serving. Serve at once.
Serves 2.

In Rome, this dessert is served flaming with cognac; warm 1–2 tablespoons cognac, pour over chocolate, and ignite.

LEMONADE WITH LEMON ICE

The piazza, center of the social life of Capri, is crammed with varicolored chairs and tables belonging to four competing restaurants. In the morning and around seven o'clock in the evening, everyone sits at tables, sips drinks, and watches the passing parade.

This lemonade combines a cooling drink with dessert.

2 lemons
Ice cubes
Granulated sugar
1/2 pint lemon ice

1. Squeeze the juice of 1 lemon into each tall glass.
2. Put ice cubes in each glass and fill two-thirds full with water. Add sugar to taste and stir well.
3. Put 1 scoop of lemon ice in each glass and serve at once.
Serves 2.

PAPAYA–STRAWBERRY ICE

1 small or 1/2 large papaya
1 lemon
1/2 package (about 5 ounces) frozen strawberries

1. Peel and seed papaya; slice into a blender and squeeze in juice of lemon.
2. Cut frozen berries into chunks and add to blender. Purée until smooth.
3. Pour into a shallow dish and serve immediately or place in freezer until serving time.
Serves 2.

ESPRESSO WITH ICE CREAM

Combines dessert with coffee.

Crushed ice
2 cups hot strong coffee
1/2 pint vanilla ice cream

1. Put crushed ice in 2 tall glasses and pour 1 cup of hot coffee into each glass.
2. Put 1 scoop of vanilla ice cream in each glass and serve at once.
Serves 2.

VENETIAN ORANGES

In Venice you can look out to see wonderful landscapes and a pattern of islands; the colors everywhere are misty pinks and terra-cottas. The shell pink of the Doges' Palace changes with each shift of light.

1 cup water
1/2 cup granulated sugar
2 medium-size oranges
2 tablespoons orange liqueur (optional)

1. Combine water and sugar in a saucepan; grate rind of oranges into pan. Place pan over high heat, stirring to dissolve sugar. Boil rapidly for 5 minutes to form a syrup.
2. With a sharp knife, peel oranges carefully so no white remains.
3. When syrup thickens, remove pan from heat. Place oranges in syrup, turning them over so the oranges are well coated. Leave them in the syrup for 2–3 minutes.
4. Remove oranges to a dish; add orange liqueur to syrup and pour over oranges.
5. Refrigerate until ready to serve. Serves 2.

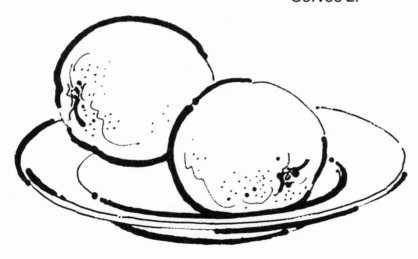

ALMOND TORTE CAPRI

Haunting Capri has light, airy clouds; the misty sky and calm sea seem to reflect every shade of green and blue. I will never forget the full moon dropping moonbeams on the tranquil water. This almond torte, a favorite on Capri, is in every baker's window; I have never found it anywhere else.

2 large eggs, at room temperature
1/2 cup almonds or walnuts
1/2 cup granulated sugar
1/4 cup powdered cocoa
1/4 cup powdered sugar

Preheat oven to 375°F
1. Break eggs into a blender and mix for about 1 minute until light and foamy. Add almonds and blend until finely ground.
2. Add granulated sugar to blender and mix well. Stir cocoa in 1 tablespoon at a time, blending well.
3. Pour batter into a buttered 6 X 9-inch pan. Bake in *preheated* oven about 12 minutes, or until cake comes away from sides of pan. Do not overcook or the torte will be dry.
4. Remove torte from oven and dust with powdered sugar while still warm. Cut into squares and serve at room temperature.
Makes 8 squares.

EASY MACAROONS

The Italians invented macaroons; they are easy to make and perfect with wine for dessert.

1 large egg
1/2 cup granulated sugar
1 tablespoon unsalted butter
1/2 cup almonds
1 lemon or orange
1/2 cup all-purpose flour

Preheat oven to 375°F
1. Break egg into a blender and mix for a few seconds. Add sugar, butter, and almonds and blend until almonds are finely ground, about 1 minute.
2. Cut 3 thin strips of lemon rind into blender, add juice of lemon, and purée until smooth. Stir flour in 1 tablespoon at a time. Turn on blender to mix well.
3. Drop batter in small rounds from a teaspoon onto a buttered oven sheet. Bake in *preheated* oven for 8–10 minutes until lightly golden. Serve at room temperature.
Makes about 14 small cookies.

HAZELNUT BARS

A favorite in Rome.

1 large egg
1 cup firmly packed brown sugar
1 tablespoon unsalted butter
2 heaping tablespoons all-purpose flour
1/2 cup hazelnuts or walnuts

Preheat oven to 375°F
1. Break egg into a blender and mix for a few seconds. Add sugar and butter; mix for 1 minute until light and creamy.
2. Stir flour into blender. Add hazelnuts and blend briefly to chop nuts coarsely.
3. Pour batter into a buttered 6 X 9-inch pan. Bake in *preheated* oven for 12–15 minutes, or until batter comes away from sides of pan.
4. Remove from oven, let cool, and cut into squares.
Makes 12 squares.

DELICIOUS BROWNIES

Try these rich chocolate delights; they
will melt in your mouth.

2-1/2 ounces (2 large squares)
    semisweet chocolate
4 tablespoons unsalted butter
1 cup firmly packed brown sugar
2 eggs
1/2 teaspoon vanilla extract
1/2 cup all-purpose flour
1/4 cup walnuts

Preheat oven to 375°F
1. Put chocolate in a small bowl and
place in oven for a few minutes to melt.
2. Put butter, sugar, eggs, and vanilla in
a blender and mix until smooth.
3. Stir flour into blender 1 tablespoon
at a time. Add melted chocolate and
walnuts and blend for 2–3 seconds.
4. Spread batter in a well-buttered 6 X
9-inch pan. Bake in *preheated* oven
for 12–15 minutes; be careful not to
overcook.
5. Remove from oven; when cool, cut
into squares.
Makes 20 small squares.

BREAD PUDDING

This elegant dessert is quickly and inexpensively made. To preserve the delicate flavor, cook gently.

3 slices coarse white bread
Butter, at room temperature
2 large whole eggs, plus 1 egg yolk
1/2 cup milk
1/2 cup heavy cream
1/2 teaspoon vanilla extract
1 orange
1/4 cup firmly packed brown sugar

Preheat oven to 350°F
1. Toast bread in *preheated* oven until golden brown; butter one side of each piece of toast.
2. Break whole eggs and egg yolk into a bowl; beat lightly with a whisk or egg beater until blended.
3. Add milk, cream, and vanilla; grate rind of orange into bowl. Stir the custard until well combined.
4. Spread sugar evenly on bottom of a 6 X 9-inch oven dish. Arrange toast, buttered sides up, on sugar; pour custard over toast.
5. Bake pudding in *preheated* oven for 12–15 minutes until custard is *just* set. Be careful not to overcook; remove pudding from oven before it is completely firm.
6. Serve pudding at room temperature; the brown sugar on the bottom of the dish forms a delicious sauce.
Serves 2 generously.

ROMAN SCONES

On a cold day the tea room on the Piazza di Spagna is filled with shoppers and walkers, pausing for a hot cup of tea, chocolate, or coffee with a plate of buttery scones or a sweet. Some of the most elegant and opulent shops in the world are on the streets in this area, with luxurious furs, fine silks, soft leathers, jewels fit for a king. Nearby is an open market with stalls of fresh vegetables and fruit; a block away is a food shop filled with freshly baked bread, cheese, and other wonderful Italian delicacies to take home.

1 cup all-purpose flour
1 teaspoon baking powder
4 tablespoons unsalted butter
3 tablespoons milk, or as needed
1/4 cup dried currants

Preheat oven to 375°F
1. Combine flour, baking powder, and butter in a mixing bowl. With a knife, cut butter into dry ingredients until well mixed and the consistency of coarse crumbs.
2. Add currants; stir 2 tablespoons milk into mixture. With your fingers, quickly form dough into a ball; add more milk if needed to make a soft, workable dough.
3. Pat dough into a flat round on a buttered oven sheet; cut into quarters with a knife.
4. Bake in *preheated* oven for 10–12 minutes until golden brown. Serve hot. Makes 4 scones.

SICILIAN COOKIES

Sicily raises luscious crops of citrus fruits—beautiful blood-red oranges and fragrant lemons. Cakes, cookies, and breads are made with chopped fruit.

1 lemon
1/2 cup granulated sugar
1 egg
4 tablespoons unsalted butter, at room temperature
1 scant cup all-purpose flour
1 teaspoon baking powder

Preheat oven to 350°F
1. Cut lemon into quarters, discard seeds, and place in a blender to purée lemon.
2. Add sugar, egg, and butter to blender and mix until smooth.
3. Combine flour and baking powder and stir into blender 1 tablespoon at a time. Turn on blender to mix well.
4. Drop batter in small rounds from a teaspoon onto a buttered oven sheet. Bake in *preheated* oven for 5–6 minutes until golden. Cool and remove to a plate.
Makes about 18 small cookies.

This is a tart cookie; dust with powdered sugar, if you like a sweet contrast. You can make as few cookies as you wish, and refrigerate or freeze the remaining batter for another time.

RICOTTA PANCAKES

In summer I went early to market before the heat of the day; the fresh produce is unloaded and placed in stalls. The white ricotta sells quickly; watermelons look cool cut in half, the pale pink inside rimmed with dark green edges.

1 egg
1/4 cup sour cream
1/2 cup ricotta cheese
2 tablespoons all-purpose flour
2 tablespoons unsalted butter
1/2 cup red currant jelly
1 lemon

1. Put egg, sour cream, and ricotta in a blender and mix for a few seconds until smooth.
2. Place ricotta mixture in a bowl; stir in flour, blending well.
3. Melt 1 tablespoon butter in a sauté pan or skillet over medium heat. When hot, add 1 tablespoonful of batter to pan for each pancake. Cook until golden brown and pancakes turn easily, about 1 minute on each side. Remove to a plate when done.
4. Lower heat, add remaining 1 table-spoon butter to pan, and make pancakes with remaining batter.
5. To make sauce, heat jelly in a small pan over medium heat and squeeze in juice of lemon. Simmer for 2 minutes, stirring as jelly melts.
6. Serve pancakes warm or at room temperature with hot currant jelly sauce. Serves 2.

RICOTTA DESSERT

The Sicilians love ices and pastries; desserts are often a mixture of sweetened ricotta and bits of chopped chocolate.

1 cup ricotta cheese
1/2 cup heavy cream
2 tablespoons granulated sugar
1 tablespoon brandy
2 tablespoons grated semisweet
  chocolate

1. Combine ricotta, cream, sugar, and brandy in a blender and mix until smooth.
2. Place ricotta mixture in a bowl and sprinkle with grated chocolate. Chill until serving time.
Serves 2.

GORGONZOLA CREAM

I first had this heavenly cheese in Venice. Built on the water, Venice mirrors and reflects everything. All of the city seems to be a backdrop for drama, grand opera, intrigue. The smell of the sea is always in the air.

1/4 pound gorgonzola cheese
1/4 pound mascarpone cheese
2 tablespoons heavy cream
10 fresh basil leaves (no stems)
1/4 cup pine nuts (optional)

1. Combine gorgonzola, mascarpone, cream, and basil leaves in a blender and blend until smooth.
2. Place cheese mixture in a bowl and stir in pine nuts. Serve at room temperature.
Serves 2 generously.

Serve with thin slices of crusty toasted bread.

WINES in Italy take their names from the district where the grapes are grown, or from the name of the grape they are made with. The vintage is not important, since most Italian wines are meant to be drunk young, usually within three to five years.

Italy has an enormous range of climates, from the northern alps to sunny Sicily, from the seacoast to the rolling inland hills, from the plains to the mountains. Vines grow almost everywhere, resulting in a huge variety of wines.

It is a challenge to sample as many wines as possible while visiting Italy, for many of the local wines are usually not shipped out of the country; most cannot even be found in other regions within the country. Everybody with a piece of land grows grapes and makes his own wine; most wine is drunk locally and comes from small, private vineyards.

The Italian seems to believe wine is a pleasure to be enjoyed, and so wine is treated casually, without mystique. A bottle of wine is placed on the table for meals, along with a bottle of water.

It was years ago, but I still remember with pleasure a meal in Sardinia starting with a dry sherrylike wine, followed by a pasta stuffed with cream cheese flavored with wild herbs and served with pitchers of a local young white wine; and finishing with a crispy pancake filled with bitter dark honey, and a Sardinian liqueur made from myrtle blossoms and many other flowers. The wine and food were perfect for the day in the open air with the sun sparkling on the sea. The farmer had only a few vines; the wines were made in small quantities and consumed on the spot: wine is to drink for pleasure, to lift the spirit.

Around Rome, the grapes grow on the Alban hills. The light red and white Castelli Romani wines produced here go well with Roman food. Frascati, the best of the whites, is named for the town where it is made, only minutes away from Rome and worth the trip just to have lunch and to drink a glass of this pleasant wine at its source.

One recent sunny October day I drove with a friend from Rome to Orvieto, crossing the Paglia River along the way. Orvieto is a medieval town built on high rocks overlooking the green hills of Umbria. Standing in the town, high above the fields, I could see the rolling vineyards where the grapes are grown

to make the Orvieto wines. Made in both dry (*secco*) and sweet (*abboccato*) versions, these pale-golden wines were once enjoyed by the Etruscans. Today they are considered to be among the best white wines produced in Italy.

A few weeks later we drove about forty miles north of Venice into the countryside near Treviso; we saw immaculately tended hillsides with grapes growing on trellises and pergolas. We stopped at a lively country market to sample cheeses and to drink Prosecco, the honey-scented golden wine for which the area is most famous, and the sparkling version, Prosecco Spumante. These white wines make perfect accompaniments to the local sausage, salami, and crusty bread.

The vineyards around Verona, one of the largest wine-producing regions in Italy, yield some of the country's best wines. Valpolicella and Bardolino are light, gentle reds, wonderful with the local tortellini, green pasta, and ravioli stuffed with fresh garden vegetables. All are served with cream and butter sauces, and the rice is often cooked with saffron.

The wine regions of Friuli-Venezia Giulia, Trentino-Alto Adige, and the

Veneto form the most important white-wine zone of Italy. The Veneto produces the pale-golden, delicately flavored Soave, one of the best Italian wines. The Merlot grape from this area produces a soft red wine. The Trentino-Alto region, stretching from the end of Lake Garda to the terraced foothills of the Dolomites, has some of Italy's most dramatic vineyards. Riesling, Traminer, and Pinto grapes are the base for most of the light and fruity wines made here. The Alto Adige, the northern area of this region also known as the Italian Tyrol, formerly part of Austria, has some of the highest vineyards in Italy, with stupendous views of the Dolomite peaks. The aromatic wines produced here resemble those of Austria.

Driving through the Piedmont region, which forms the northwest border of the country, I sampled Barbera and Barolo, both full-bodied rich red wines. Some of Italy's best and most expensive wines are made from the Nebbiolo grape grown in this area: Barbaresco seems to have a bouquet of violets; Grignolino has a light nutty flavor. Asti Spumante, the sparkling wine for all festive occasions, comes from the near-by region of Valle d'Aosta.

Bologna is known for fine cooking, rich pasta dishes, hams, salamis, and

the large pink sausage, cotechino. Small rounds of pasta (tortellini, tortelloni) filled with meat or pumpkin and ricotta cheese are served in broth or with a cream sauce. The Bolognese are famous for a dish combining boiled chicken, meats, and sausage with a spicy green sauce. Desserts are confections of sweet cheese and cream drenched in brandy. Pleasant wines from the nearby vineyards include an unusual semisparkling red Lambrusco, surprisingly good with the rich local delicacies, and Trebbiano di Romagna, a light, fresh wine.

The rugged beauty of Tuscany, with the Chianti hills rising steeply above Florence, is broken by the silver gray of the olive groves. The foothills of the Apennines are lined with row upon row of vines, which ramble all over the region; nestling in these hills are about 150,000 acres of vineyards. The Etruscans made wine in their native Tuscany, as did the Romans who followed them; but it was during the Renaissance that wine making developed into an art in Florence and the nearby Chianti hills. Wine, olives, and olive oil are Tuscany's most important agricultural products today.

The Tuscan hills, half an hour from central Florence, provide an interesting drive. After going through acres of dark groves of evergreen trees, you suddenly emerge into sunlit slopes and drive past tiny secluded villages built of stone. The grapevines here are generally cultivated by the *spallièra* method, with the branches strung out vertically on lines to form neat rows and to create exposure to the sun. The climate (dry hot summers, wet autumns and winters) is ideal for grape growing. The grapes for Chianti can be grown only on hilly slopes; much of Italy is mountainous, so most of the grapes that produce Italian wines are hill grown.

The Chianti hills are in the "classico" section; Chianti country proper straddles the districts of Florence and Siena, its boundaries defined by law. The designation "classico" on a label indicates a Chianti of top quality, and the grapes must be grown in this area.

Classic Chianti wine is made from a blend of four different red and white grapes. Each wine maker has his own blend, so Chianti has a wide range of styles and personalities; but generally speaking it is a warm, earthy, robust wine. There are two basic types of Chianti, young and aged. The main characteristics of young Chianti are its freshness, lightness, and slightly bitter flavor. It must be drunk within a year or two, and is often seen in a straw-wrapped bottle. Aged Chianti is allowed to age in oak barrels for two to three years or more; the grapes must be of fine quality, and the final wine is rich, full, and complex. This is a warm, smooth wine, capable of aging for ten to twenty years. If it has had a minimum of three years' aging at the winery, it can wear the word "riserva" on its label. Aged Chianti will be found in a straight-shouldered bottle, never in straw. Look for the neck label, a black rooster framed in red signifying Chianti Classico, the sign of the best Chianti wines around Florence.

If you visit the Chianti country near Florence, you can stop at various castles and buy wine, as the Italians do, directly from the wine maker. On weekends in this region, cars can be seen with huge straw-covered jugs strapped to the roofs, going to the vineyards to fill the empty jugs with wine.

When I lived in Florence, it was an easy drive to the Adriatic seacoast to visit Ravenna and the beautiful mosaics. North of Ravenna, near Ancona, the light Verdicchio wines are grown. I always enjoy this slightly bitter wine with the fresh seafood dishes.

In late summer I drove to Naples to take the boat to Capri. Along the way I saw fruit and olive trees growing in widely spaced rows, with vegetables (beans, cabbage, broccoli) planted between them; garlands of grapevines climbed over and were supported by the trees; three crops can be harvested from the same land each year.

In Naples I had a glass of slightly sparkling, light-red Gragnano with a crisp pizza, and I tried the white Falerno, known and liked by the ancient Greek poets. On Capri I saw the small Greco grapevines straggling over the hillsides; they are used to make the local wines. The white wines of Capri and Ischia are wonderful with light summer meals.

Sicily has a beautiful countryside of olive, lemon, and orange groves, a lushness the English have found appealing for centuries. Driving, you can see some of the world's largest vineyards, endless fields of grain and corn, and in the spring, flowers blooming everywhere. Wine is Sicily's most important agricultural crop after citrus fruits. There are red and white wines, and the well-known sweet dessert wine, Marsala.

SERVING WINES

In Italy, wine is made to drink with the meal; the selection of the wine plays an important part in the enjoyment of the meal. When choosing a wine, remember one basic rule: light wines go best with light foods and heavy wines go best with heavy foods. You can serve white wine with almost any food; when you are serving red meat, you may prefer to serve white wine before the meal and red wine with the meat. If you are serving more than one wine on the same occasion, serve the dry, light wines before the sweet wines, and the young wines before the older ones.

Serve white wines chilled about one hour in the refrigerator, as wine becomes tasteless with too much chilling. Serve red wines at cool room temperature.

Store leftover wine in the refrigerator with the cork tightly replaced; an opened bottle will keep about a week. I use my opened wine for cooking.

The classic tulip shape is a good choice for one all-purpose wineglass. Be certain the glass is large enough to allow the flavor of the wine to develop; wine is made for drinking, not for sipping.

A SIMPLE WINE GUIDE

Light and medium white wines are good with fish, seafood, veal, chicken, pasta, omelets, and a mild cheese like bel paese. Examples are Frascati, Orvieto, Soave, Verdicchio, and Pinot Grigio.

Light and medium red wines are good with pork, light beef dishes, tomato-sauced pastas, well-seasoned dishes, and a rich, piquant cheese like fontina. Examples are Bardolino, Chianti, Lambrusco, Valpolicella, and Barbera.

Robust red wines are good with steak, roast beef, liver, roast turkey, game, and strong cheeses like gorgonzola and provolone. Examples are Barbaresco, Barolo, and Chianti Classico Riserva.

Sparkling and dessert wines are good with fruit, desserts, nuts, and glacéed chestnuts. Sparkling wines, *spumante* (foaming), are often served for celebrations. The very dry types are known as *brut*; when only slightly sparkling, the wines are *frizzante*. Examples are Asti Spumante, Spumante Brut, Prosecco, and Marsala.

APERITIVO: AT THE BEGINNING

An *aperitivo* is a light drink served before a meal to stimulate the appetite. It is a combination of herbs, spices, blended wines, spirits, and bitters, usually low in alcohol content and with a subtle bouquet. Italians believe there are many virtues in *aperitivi,* as they contain herbs beneficial to the digestion. Some of the most popular Italian *aperitivi* are:

Campari is actually an Italian bitters. This scarlet liquid is an extract of distilled spirits and herbs; though bitter, it is refreshing when combined with ice, soda water, and lemon.

Cynar is made from artichokes, which Italians believe healthful, and especially good for the liver. Perhaps the most unusual of the *aperitivi,* with a unique sweet, slightly bitter flavor.

Fernet Branca, composed of alcohol and herbs, is an Italian cure-all for indigestion and hangovers. The cure, however, is almost worse than the ailment, as this drink is extremely bitter.

Punt e Mes is a vermouth that is both bitter and sweet. Best served over ice with soda water and a bit of lemon so the distinctive flavor can be appreciated.

Vermouth is available white, red, dry, and sweet, and is made with fortified white wines. Good over ice with a twist of lemon and a bit of soda. The Italians say a drink of vermouth relaxes the stomach and aids digestion. *Bianco secco* is dry white vermouth; *rosso* is sweet red vermouth.

White wine is perfect for serving as a light drink before a meal. White wines should be chilled in the refrigerator about one hour. You may wish to serve the same white wine you will be drinking later with your meal; a light-bodied Frascati, a fruity Pinot Grigio, or a fuller-flavored Orvieto or Verdicchio are good choices.

CAPRI SANGRIA

A walk along a path above the sea
leads to an open-air restaurant, built on
a platform of old chestnut trees looking
out over the water and the rocks below
covered with sea urchins. After a swim
in buoyant water, it is pleasant to bask
in the sun, to sip sangría; later there is
a platter of assorted shellfish and spaghetti with good Capri wine. After lunch
a boat ride takes you home.

2 cups white or red wine
1 cup mineral water
Ice cubes
1 small peach
1/2 unpeeled orange
1 lemon
Granulated sugar

1. Pour wine and water into a pitcher;
add ice cubes and stir well.
2. Peel peach; slice peach and orange
very thin into pitcher.
3. Add 2–3 thin slices lemon and squeeze
in lemon juice to taste. Add sugar to
taste and stir well.
Serves 2.

NEGRONI

2 thin slices orange
Ice cubes
1 part Punt e Mes
1 part Campari
1 part gin

1. Place an orange slice and ice cubes in each tall glass.
2. Add Punt e Mes, Campari, and gin, in equal parts; stir well.
Serves 2.

CAMPARI

3 ounces Campari
Ice cubes
1 lemon
Soda water

1. Pour Campari over ice cubes into each tall glass; squeeze in juice of lemon.
2. Add soda water and stir well.
Serves 2.

VERMOUTH AND CAMPARI APERITIVO

3 ounces sweet red vermouth
3 ounces Campari
3 ounces dry white wine
Crushed ice
Soda water
2 thin slices orange

1. In a shaker or pitcher, combine vermouth, Campari, and white wine with crushed ice and shake or stir mixture well. Pour into 2 wineglasses.
2. Add a dash of soda water to each glass and garnish with orange slices.
Serves 2.

CYNAR

Ice cubes
2 thin slices orange
3 ounces Cynar
3 ounces vodka
Sweet red vermouth

1. Place ice cubes and 1 orange slice in each tall glass.
2. Add Cynar and vodka and a dash of vermouth to each glass; stir well.
Serves 2.

TIZIANA

1 cup grapefruit juice
1 cup chilled champagne
Ice cubes
Dash bitters or grenadine

1. Pour grapefruit juice and cold champagne into a pitcher; add ice cubes.
2. Add a dash of bitters and stir well.
3. Serve in 2 chilled wineglasses.
Serves 2.

THE BELLINI

This heavenly Venetian drink is made when the small white-and-pink peach is in season.

3 small white peaches
1 lemon
Chilled champagne

1. Peel peaches and slice into a blender; squeeze in juice of lemon and purée until smooth.
2. Mix 1 part peach purée to 2 parts cold champagne in each glass.
Serves 2.

LIQUORE: AT THE END

Italians often end an evening with a *liquóre*, a sweet, fragrant liquid flavored with aromatic herbs and sugar. Some of the most popular are:

Amaretto has an almond flavor and is made fragrant with almond and apricot pits and vanilla bean.

Galliano is a pale green-gold liquid with a hint of licorice.

Frangelico has a lingering hazelnut flavor; good over ice cream.

Lemonier is made from natural lemon peel; deliciously tart and sweet.

Mandarinetto di Sicilia has the taste of mandarin oranges.

Maraschino is made from cherries; a popular flavoring for desserts.

Sambuca is a sweet anise-flavored syrup; try some in your after-dinner espresso. In Italy, Sambuca is often served with three to four coffee beans floating in the glass to be crunched as you sip; a wonderful combination—the bitter with the sweet.

MENUS for all seasons: There is an excitement in Italy that comes with each new season and its special foods. I hope the following text and menus will pass this feeling on to you.

Many of the rules for food have changed; we have greater freedom in the kitchen today. There is a new approach to eating: thought is given to the body and nutrition, much produce is in the marketplace year-round, a greater variety of imported foods are available, and there are better convenience foods for quick meals. If you shop wisely, you can have healthy meals with pure flavors all during the year.

I hope my recipes and menus will inspire your marketing, cooking, and eating.

When planning meals, *remember:*

- To avoid repetition of ingredients; if using eggs or wine in one dish, don't repeat in another.
- To use fresh, in-season products as often as possible for good health.
- To balance your meals; opposites attract: team bland with spicy, sweet with tart, crisp with smooth.
- To combine a rich dish with a plain one, a complicated recipe with a simple one.
- To be flexible when marketing; try new foods, your meals will be more interesting.
- To enjoy a glass of wine with your meal.

Salute !

ITALY IN SPRING

Spring means the winter bitterness is gone; Rome is filled with flowers, trees with new green leaves, flying swallows, and fountains sparkling in the sunshine. The sun warms ancient churches, marble palaces, terraced gardens, and people sitting in outdoor cafes. When Rome celebrates its birthday on the night of April twenty-first, the Campodoglio, hillside capitol of old Rome, is lighted with thousands of bright candles that look like fireflies in the soft spring evening.

Romans know spring has arrived when the plump and tender artichokes reach the open markets and restaurant tables.

There are stalls of fresh cheeses, wild strawberries from the Alban hills, baby lamb, thin asparagus, small peas and carrots, and special green grasses for salads.

During the warm days there are tours of famous Florentine gardens with water-wreathed fountains. In Rome it is pleasant to walk in the Botanical Gardens, between the rows of citrus trees in terra-cotta pots, past a grotto, and up stone steps with moss-covered balustrades.

SPRING MENUS

Assorted Vegetables with Sauce
Risotto with Asparagus
Sicilian Cookies

Lamb on Skewers with Herbs
Cauliflower Salad
Peaches with Wine

Crostini
Chicken on Skewers
Grated Carrots
Strawberries with Vinegar

Fresh Pea Soup
Braised Salmon
Easy Macaroons

Country Omelet
Sicilian Tomatoes
Gorgonzola Cream with crusty bread

Black Olives with Lemon Slices
Pork Chops Marsala
Green Salad with Herb Dressing
Roman Scones

ITALY IN SUMMER

Summer in Italy means hot days and long warm nights. Many Italians drive to the sea to enjoy the sun, to relax in uncomplicated surroundings with pine trees, flowers, and paths for walking. On weekends boats to Capri and Portofino are crowded; the small patches of sand and rocks are colorful with umbrellas and bronzed bodies.

There is much to do in Rome in the evening: the open-air opera in the luxurious third-century Baths of Caracalla, and concerts at night in the Borghese Gardens. There is also Greek theater recreated in the Villa Giulia with Etruscan art treasures and the full moon as a setting.

The season for outdoor dining has arrived. The summer dishes are light pastas combined with vegetables, fresh seafood, luscious peaches and ripe figs, green basil and mint, deep-red tomatoes, and fruit ices. During the warm weather all restaurants have cool leafy extensions where eating is a pleasure under a flower-covered arbor with flickering candles.

SUMMER MENUS

Prawns with Basil
Pasta with Eggplant Sauce
Papaya-Strawberry Ice

Sesame Chicken
Grated Squash Sauté
Peaches and Figs with Cream

Turkey with Tuna Sauce
Green Salad with Lemon Dressing
Lemonade with Lemon Ice

Tongue Salad
Semolina Gnocchi
Espresso with Ice Cream

Penne with Zucchini
Italian Sausage Capri
Almond Torte Capri

Poached Halibut with Caper Sauce
Baked Tomatoes
Ricotta Pancakes

ITALY IN AUTUMN

Autumn brings warm days and golden light; these are the lazy days before the crisp air and rain of November. Autumn in the marketplace means abundance; a wide variety of fruits and vegetables are on display. The bees and wasps swarm over baskets of amber grapes just picked and brought from the vineyards. There are boxes of russet pears, late peaches, persimmons, and pomegranates with green leaves.

The light dishes disappear with the heat of summer; eating habits change as the cooler weather gives a keener edge to the appetite. The autumnal flavors are richer, earthier than the more delicate summer tastes. The vegetables are different—giant squash, small leaves of spinach, tender fennel, and *arugula* for salads. There are chestnuts, game, huge mushrooms (*porcini*), and truffles; even the herbs are different—sage, rosemary, thyme, and bay. Rice, beans, and root vegetables are made into soups and combined with sauces to make heavier meals.

Italians go to the country to see the change of season and to eat in small, rustic restaurants. Autumn menus offer gnocchi with fresh herbs, vegetable puddings, small birds, pork cooked in sour-sweet sauce, cakes and cookies made with nuts, and thick fruit purées with ice cream.

AUTUMN MENUS

Ricotta Gnocchi
Artichokes, Roman Style
Persimmon Purée with Vanilla Ice Cream

Veal Chops with Brandy
Mushroom, Celery, and Fontina Salad
Bread Pudding

Red and Yellow Peppers
Kidneys with Walnuts
Fennel with Oil and Lemon
Chestnuts Cooked in Wine

Risotto with Pink Shrimp Sauce
Broccoli and Zucchini
Sliced Frozen Persimmon

Scallops with Parsley Sauce
Celery Purée
Venetian Oranges

Chicken with Mustard Sauce
Endives and grapes with Walnut Oil Dressing
Ricotta Dessert

ITALY IN WINTER

Winter in northern Italy is cold; the marble floors are like ice and the harsh winds chill the bones, penetrating leather and fur. Milan has dense fog, and the season of opera and concerts is underway at La Scala. Venice in the cold months stands in rain and mist; the seabirds swoop and flutter above the black water, sweeping in and out of the dim light. Many Italians travel to the Dolomites to celebrate Christmas and the New Year in the snow-covered alps.

On Christmas Day an elaborate meal is served midday. Usually the festive meal starts with champagne, followed by antipasto, tortellini, chestnuts, and turkey. There is always *torrone*, the traditional Christmas nougat candy, and *panettone*, a cakelike bread baked with currants and candied fruit. On New Year's Eve, Italians wear red for good luck, and a stew of lentils is the traditional dish served on New Year's Day to insure a prosperous new year.

During the cold winter months, Romans and Florentines visit small restaurants with blazing fireplaces to eat golden polenta, oxtail stew, white beans with spinach and walnuts, thick soups, and boiled meats with a green sauce, all hot, full-flavored dishes to warm the body and sustain the spirit.

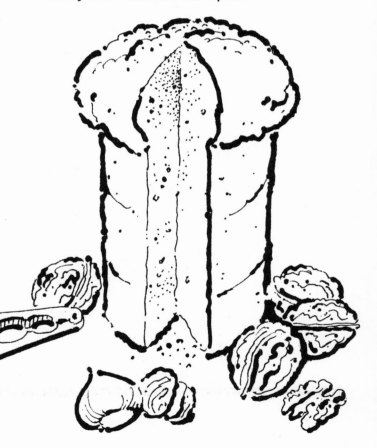

WINTER MENUS

Pork Cooked in Milk
Sliced Oranges with Anchovy Dressing
Hazelnut Bars

Artichoke Salad
Zucchini Pudding with Tomato Sauce
Pears Marsala

Polenta with Cheese
Spinach with Oil and Lemon
Coffee Ice Cream with Chestnuts

Spinach Soup with Cornmeal
Crab Legs with Mushrooms
Bel paese with pears and grapes

Baked Stuffed Mushrooms
Poached Beef with Two Sauces
Delicious Brownies

CHRISTMAS MENU

Deviled Chestnuts
Turkey Breast with Foie Gras Sauce
Green Beans with Cheese
Chocolate Sauce with Chocolate Ice Cream
flamed with cognac

INDEX

EMALEE SALA CHAPMAN, author of the popular *Fifteen Minute Meals,* developed a taste for good food and wine from her Italian parents while growing up in California. She later lived in Florence, where she pursued her interest in cooking. She decided to learn to cook to re-create some of the glorious food she had known at home and in Italy. Mrs. Chapman opened a cooking school in San Francisco in 1969; she is a frequent contributor of food articles to national magazines, including *House and Garden, Family Circle,* and *Self Magazine.* A graduate of Stanford University, she has also studied at the University of Florence, Le Cordon Bleu, and Maxim's Cooking Courses in Paris.

ALICE HARTH, an award-winning San Francisco illustrator and graphic designer and lover of good food and travel, met Emalee Chapman while attending her cooking classes. This meeting led to her designing and illustrating Mrs. Chapman's first book, *Fifteen Minute Meals.* Alice Harth's design clients have included food corporations, restaurants, magazines, and book publishers. She currently teaches a design-illustration course at City College of San Francisco. A native of California, she studied fine arts and design at the University of California at Los Angeles.